Thomas Edison

Thomas Edison

Jan Adkins

DK Publishing

LONDON, NEW YORK, MUNICH,
MELBOURNE, AND DELHI

Editor : Beth Landis Hester
Publishing Director : Beth Sutinis
Designer : Mark Johnson Davies
Managing Art Editor : Michelle Baxter
Production Controller : Jen Lockwood
DTP Coordinator : Kathy Farias
Photo Research : Anne Burns Images

First American Edition, 2009

09 10 11 12 13 10 9 8 7 6 5 4 3 2
Published in the United States
by DK Publishing
375 Hudson Street
New York, New York 10014

DK books are available at special discounts
when purchased in bulk for sales promotions,
premiums, fund-raising,
or educational use. For details, contact:

DK Publishing Special Markets
375 Hudson Street
New York, New York 10014
SpecialSales@dk.com

A catalog record for this book is available
from the Library of Congress.

ISBN 978-0-7566-5207-4 (Paperback)
ISBN 978-0-7566-5206-7 (Hardcover)

Printed and bound in China
by South China Printing Co., Ltd.

Discover more at
www.dk.com

Contents

Prologue

Jubilee of Light

It was the celebration of a turning point in human history. The elderly man at the center of the commemoration, one of the most recognizable faces in the world, sat quietly. His suit was rumpled, his hair barely combed. He smiled but he didn't hear the applause or the grandiloquent speeches.

A replica of Edison's incandescent bulb shows the same socket and connections as the original.

Thomas Alva Edison was not quite part of the hubbub because he was almost completely deaf.

He was being honored for bringing the world out of darkness. Henry Ford, the industrialist who mounted the massive event, called it the "Golden Jubilee of Light," the 50th anniversary of Edison's invention of the lightbulb. (Technically, Edison didn't invent the lightbulb—but that fact was overlooked.)

As the evening wore on, the old man wore down. He roused the strength to leave the banquet hall with Ford, his old assistant Francis Jehl, President Herbert Hoover, and a radio reporter. It was a short walk to the laboratory he had built in Menlo Park, New Jersey, even though the celebration was being held in Ford's hometown of Dearborn, Michigan. Edison's laboratory had been brought stick by stick from New Jersey. In the lab, all the original equipment was in its place: the lead-and–sulfuric acid batteries, the vacuum pump, the glass globe holding a carbonized bamboo filament.

Edison and Jehl connected the electrical contacts to the battery as they had 50 years before, in 1879. Light blazed in the dim laboratory. In deep, biblical tones, the radio announcer spoke: "And Edison said, 'Let there be light!'"

Afterward Edison's wife, Mina, arranged for a glass of warm milk, which revived him enough to sit through more speeches. Edison finally rose to speak. He thanked everyone for their good wishes and said he was especially happy that science was the real subject of the evening. Then he bid them good night. He sat down, pale with the effort, and was taken away by Mina and President Hoover's physician. He would spend the next few days in Ford's home, in bed. He insisted, "I am tired of all the glory, I want to get back to work."

Work, almost constant work, at all hours of day and night, had been the current running through his extraordinary life. Since he left his home at 12 to hawk newspapers and candy on the Grand Trunk Railroad, Tom Edison had been working, hustling, discovering, inventing.

Now Edison, a white-haired old man, was one of the most famous men in the world. Henry Ford said, "To find a man who has not benefited by Edison and who is not in debt to

him, it would be necessary to go deep into the jungle.
I hold him to be our greatest American."

To the American public, he was like a saint, or the nation's kindly, brilliant uncle. He held more than 1,000 patents for things basic to modern life. He seemed to have invented the bustling commercial age of the 20th century. His industry reached into virtually every home in the Western world.

Edison was America's chosen scientist. He was consulted by the press and government about every new development in science and technology. He was even asked for his opinion on religion, marriage, and politics. The press loved Tom Edison; he was always good for a quote.

There were some who didn't like him. Some thought he took the credit for his employees' work. Others complained he was a ruthless businessman who wouldn't stop at crushing rival companies. One of his scientific rivals, the compulsively clean Nikola Tesla, said that Edison "lived in utter disregard of the most elementary rules of hygiene," and that "he would have died

Edison, Henry Ford, and Francis Jehl reenact Edison's succesful experiment from 50 years earlier.

from consequences of sheer neglect" without the care of his wife. Of Edison's hit-and-miss form of research, Tesla said, "If Edison had a needle to find in a haystack, he would proceed at once with the diligence of the bee to examine straw after straw until he found the object of his search . . . a little theory and calculation would have saved him ninety percent of his labor."

Edison wasn't a saint, especially when it came to business matters. He was a good and generous friend but touchy about insults, and

Ford's Historic Village

One of Henry Ford's lasting legacies is his 80-acre historic Greenfield Village, which is filled with more than 80 historic buildings. Visitors can walk into a courthouse where Abraham Lincoln practiced law, see the house where Noah Webster wrote the first American dictionary, or ride behind a 19th-century steam engine. Edison's lab, complete with working machines and with real New Jersey red clay beneath it, is one of the main attractions. Edison described the exhibit as "99.95% accurate."
"What about the other five hundredths?" asked Ford.
Edison shook his head,
"We never kept it this neat."

he could hold a grudge for years. He didn't have the grasp of theory and mathematics we expect from our scientists. But in an age teeming with brilliant men revealing wonders, Thomas Edison shone brighter than the rest. As he sat at the Jubilee, his deafness walled out the clamor of the crowd. But a private, inner wall, carefully constructed by Edison himself, kept the world at a distance and prevented anyone from really knowing this complex, moody, brilliant, contradictory man.

chapter
1
Foolish Questions

Running against the grain was an Edison family tradition. John Edison, Thomas's great-grandfather, stood against American Independence. He and his brother Ogden enlisted as scouts for the British during the American Revolution and were captured in 1777 by General Washington's troops. The brothers refused to swear allegiance to the United States and were sentenced to be hung for high treason, but relatives who had fought with Washington managed to save them. At the war's end in 1783, John's property was seized, and he and other pro-British families were deported to Canada. John's son Samuel fought for the British against U.S. troops in the War of 1812.

Sam Edison would pass along a tradition of adventure and resourcefulness to his youngest son, while gentle Nancy nurtured him.

In 1837, John's fiery grandson, Samuel Edison, Jr., was involved in a failed rebellion against British rule in Canada. Rebellion was a capital offense in Canada, so Sam left his wife and children behind and fled on foot, 80 miles (129 km) in two and a half wintry days, crossing the frozen St. Clair River to safety in the United States.

Sam Edison was big, six foot one (185 cm), had a gift for gab, and didn't know quite what he wanted to do. He'd been an innkeeper in Canada and had even tried work as a tailor. Seeking a fresh place with opportunities, he settled in Milan, Ohio, a bustling little town on the Huron River, about eight miles (13 km) from Lake Erie. A canal had been built to make the twisty river navigable. This made Milan a port in the heart of wheat-growing country. Farmers brought tons of grain to Milan to be loaded onto Lake Erie schooners and shipped

Memories of Milan

Thomas Edison's earliest memories were of this bustling little town striving to become a city. From the Edison home, he would have seen his father's shingle mill, a tannery, grain elevators for storing wheat and corn, smoking blacksmith forges, a waterwheel and mill-race, a steam-powered flour mill with a plume of white vapor, a covered bridge, a distillery, and shops for supplies. In 1850, the young Edison also witnessed a wagon train pausing in Milan on the way to the California gold strike.

Manifest Destiny

In 1836, the Republic of Texas had won its independence from Mexico. It was taken into the Union in 1845, a bold act that sparked the Mexican-American War. Many Americans (including Abraham Lincoln and John Quincy Adams) objected to the war and to the popular idea of Manifest Destiny, which stated that the United States was destined to expand from the Atlantic to the Pacific.

to the East. Shipyards rose to build more schooners. Milan had become a prosperous town.

After settling in Milan, Sam decided to start a shingle-making business. His friend Captain Alva Bradley barged cedar logs across Lake Erie and up the Huron. Sam sawed and split them into "shakes" to cover houses and roofs. On one of his barge trips, Captain Bradley brought Sam's family down from Canada: his wife, Nancy Elliott Edison, and their four children—Marion, William, Harriet, and Carlile.

Thomas Alva Edison was introduced to the world on February 11, 1847. He was named "Thomas" after his father's brother and "Alva" after Captain Bradley. His family called him "Al," and he was a handful. He was so curious about the world that he got in trouble right and left. He was so fascinated by a group of big grain elevators that he once fell in and disappeared beneath the grain. He was yanked out before he smothered. He fell into the Milan Canal several times. He was even found sitting on a straw nest of his own making, trying to hatch a clutch of chicken and goose eggs.

Four-year-old Al Edison is stylishly dressed in this early photograph.

Al was especially curious about the nearby workshop of Sam Winchester, whom townspeople called the "Mad Miller of Milan." Neighbors couldn't believe Winchester was neglecting his flour-milling business to build a passenger balloon. He'd already burned down his first mill while generating hydrogen gas for an earlier balloon experiment. Al returned again and again to Winchester's place, even after his father whipped him with a hazel switch and told him to stay away. Then, one day, Sam Winchester's big balloon actually inflated. The happy miller rose into the air, triumphant, and floated out over Lake Erie until he disappeared. He was never seen again.

Little Al Edison asked so many questions that townspeople

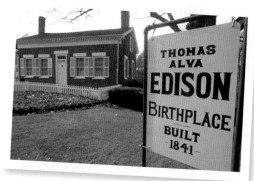

Jack-of-all-trades Sam Edison built this Milan, Ohio, home, where Al was born.

THOMAS ALVA EDISON BIRTHPLACE BUILT 1841

Young Al, shown here at age eight with his sister Tannie (Harriet Ann), was the youngest of Edison children.

thought he was odd like Sam Winchester—perhaps even slow-witted. Sam Edison was embarrassed by his youngest son's "foolish questions." When Sam answered those questions with "I don't know," Al would ask an even more infuriating question: "Why don't you know?" He didn't go to school because he was often sick, and he spent many days at home, but he loved books. He'd been taught to read by his mother, who had been a teacher in Canada.

One day, Al built an experimental fire in his father's barn . . . and burned it down. This was entirely too

A coal-burning steam engine travels the rails near Port Huron, Michigan.

This bird's-eye view of Port Huron shows the canal in the center, and a train steaming along the far left side.

much for Sam, who called his neighbors together and took Al to Milan's central square to give him a humiliating public whipping.

Edison was always respectful of his father, but their relationship was never warm. "My father thought I was stupid, and I almost decided I must be a dunce," he later explained.

Meanwhile, Sam was having problems of his own. In 1853, a railroad was built along the shore of Lake Erie, allowing farmers to deliver their grain and produce to local railroad depots. Milan's canal port began to shrivel, and Sam Edison found it hard to support his family.

Sam moved his family north to Port Huron, Michigan. At the time, the area was frontier territory, and Al was delighted to see real Erie and Potawatomi Indians, in feathered headgear, paddling canoes.

At Port Huron, Al entered a classroom for the first time. Reverend G. B. Engle ran a one-room school with tight discipline and no nonsense. He tried to correct Tom's daydreaming ways and useless questions with a leather strap. Three months later, however, Al was at the bottom of

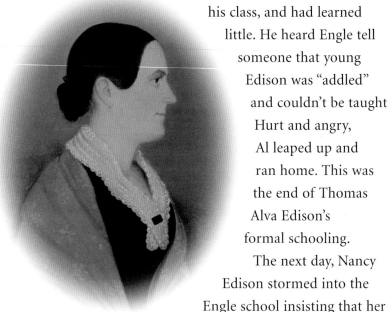

his class, and had learned little. He heard Engle tell someone that young Edison was "addled" and couldn't be taught. Hurt and angry, Al leaped up and ran home. This was the end of Thomas Alva Edison's formal schooling.

The next day, Nancy Edison stormed into the Engle school insisting that her son was anything but addled.

Nancy Elliott Edison was a kind, supportive, and adoring mother to her unusual son.

He was a wonderfully imaginative and intelligent child, and Engle was a failure as a teacher. She would teach her fine son without his help!

Actually, the family could do without the expense of school. Sam's businesses never went well, so in addition to household chores Nancy did piecework—sewing, crocheting, and weaving—to bring in money. But she still found time to devote to Al, her only child left at home after the death of three of his siblings. She introduced him to *The Decline and Fall of the Roman Empire,* the plays of Shakespeare, and the novels of Charles Dickens. Al became a rapid, hungry reader, advancing far beyond his age level. Nancy pointed his fierce curiosity at the world of words, and he tore off in pursuit of knowledge in every direction. Later, Thomas Edison would fondly talk about his mother's influence to a reporter at the *New York World:*

> I did not have my mother very long but in that length of time she cast over me an influence which has lasted all of my life. The good effects of her early training I can never lose. If it had not been for her appreciation and her faith in me at a critical time in my experience, I should very likely never have become an inventor . . . She believed that many of the Boys who turned out badly . . . would have become valuable citizens if they had been handled in the right way when they were young.

At the age of 10, Al discovered science. His mother gave him a science book filled with experiments, and he performed every one. His mother then gave him a scientific dictionary and he began more experiments. Soon, what little pocket money he was given was going toward chemicals from the pharmacy, wire, scraps of metal for batteries, test tubes, and bottles.

In those days, batteries consisted of "wet-cell" jars of sulfuric acid, which tended to spill—right onto Nancy's floor and furniture. The Edison lab was banished to the basement, where Al tried new mixes and built new machines. Nancy

"My mother was the making of me."

–Thomas Edison

The telegraph lines stretching across the vast American continent were the technical wonders of Al Edison's childhood.

protected her furniture but encouraged her son, sensing that he would find his own direction by following his curiosity. "My mother was the making of me," Edison later said. "She understood me; she let me follow my bent."

His father was less understanding. Sam remembered later, "He spent the greater part of his time in the cellar. He did not share to any extent the sports of his neighborhood. He never knew a real boyhood like other Boys." Actually, Al did spend time having fun and playing pranks with other boys. Sam was stern but he, too, was a part of Al's education. He paid the boy a penny to read books of "serious literature" and gave him a copy of Thomas Paine's *Age of Reason*, a book that challenged the foundations of organized religion. As an old man Thomas Edison would recall, "I can still remember the flash of enlightenment that showed from [those] pages."

Still, Al continued to experiment, and things occasionally exploded in the cellar. ("He will blow us all up!" Sam Edison would shout.)

"He will blow us all up!"

–Sam Edison, speaking about his son

Al decided he needed equipment to build his own telegraph, the technological wonder of the age. But money was tight. Al and a friend planted a big garden—their crops included corn, cabbages, lettuce, onions, and peas. They hoed down weeds all summer, then sold their produce door to door from a rented horse and wagon. They made a good profit on the garden, but hoeing in the sun convinced Al that he would never become a farmer.

Al bought the equipment he'd need. Using scrap metal and stove-pipe wire, with bottlenecks nailed to trees serving as insulators, he strung a working telegraph system through the woods between his house and the house of his fellow "farmer." He learned the basics of Morse code with his scrap system.

Morse Code

To communicate over distances, people once used flags or paddles to relay messages. That was before Samuel F. B. Morse's big idea: using electricity to send messages! Using short bursts ("dots") and long bursts ("dashes"), a code was assigned to each letter and number. Commonly used letters have the simplest codes (a single "•" for E and "–" for T). Letters used less frequently have more complex codes ("– • – –" for Y). No letter uses more than four dots and dashes in its code; no number uses more than five.

chapter 2

A Budding Businessman

The Grand Trunk Railroad arrived in Port Huron in 1859, connecting the frontier city with Detroit, and from there to the eastern United States. In those days, the whistle of a locomotive rushing toward distant, unknown cities was the most romantic sound in the world. Al wanted to follow that whistle.

He was only 12 and small for his age. He had, however, an enormous supply of pluck—a combination of ambition, energy, intensity, and persistence. From this point on,

Thomas Alva Edison was always seizing opportunities, looking for advantages, and making connections.

Al soon signed onto the railroad as a "candy butcher." He wasn't paid but was allowed to keep

The pluck and humor in Edison's 14-year-old face makes it easy to see why he was a successful salesman and business hustler.

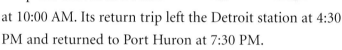

Train cars like this were Edison's place of business for several years.

everything he earned by selling newspapers and snacks. The train left Port Huron at 7:00 AM sharp and arrived in Detroit at 10:00 AM. Its return trip left the Detroit station at 4:30 PM and returned to Port Huron at 7:30 PM.

Al had trouble convincing his mother to let him take the job, but he was determined, and the family needed money. To win her over, Al made a promise to his mother: He would spend the morning and afternoon in Detroit reading, continuing his self-education.

As the train lurched away from Port Huron, little Al would walk down the aisles with a huge basket, calling out his wares: "Newspapers! Apples! Candy! Peanuts! Sandwiches!" He was tiny, loud, and so successful that he started engaging in other business on the side. He bought produce in Detroit for his fruit-and-vegetable stand in Port Huron, as well as papers for his newspaper stand. He bought berries and butter from farmers at the depots, selling them to customers in Port Huron or to railroad employees' wives. He even hired other boys to help him. He made as much as eight dollars a day, but saved most of his money and gave a dollar a day to his mother.

Al noticed things, and was always finding ways to expand his business. He usually bought 200 copies of the *Detroit Free Press* at the paper's office in the city. He soon noticed that big news sold more newspapers; a slow news day left him with unsold copies and no profit. Al began stopping in the newspaper's composing room where type was set before printing. He read the news before he placed his order.

In April 1862, one of the Civil War's bloodiest battles was fought near Shiloh, Tennessee. Casualties totaled almost 24,000 men. Al realized that the news would cause a sensation. He paid a Detroit telegrapher to send a bulletin about the battle along the rail line to be posted on the announcements blackboards at stations, so people would be eager to buy papers. Unfortunately, Al couldn't pay for all the papers he wanted, and the distribution manager

The Civil War

Americans knew that the Civil War being fought in the 1860s would change everything. If the South won independence, the "United States" would be replaced by two separate nations. If the West beyond the Rockies then declared independence from the East, as many expected, three smaller, weaker countries would result. If, on the other hand, the North won, the power of the central government would grow while states lost power. Slavery was a serious and critical issue, but much more was at stake in the war between the states.

refused him credit. So he asked Wilbur Storey, the paper's managing editor. Storey liked the nervy little kid and sent him off with a thousand papers.

Crowds were waiting for news at every station. Their relatives and friends were serving in both armies. Were they safe? At each station, Al jacked up his price. By the time he reached Port Huron, the price had risen from a few pennies to 25 cents a copy. Young Al had learned something about the power of the press.

This replica of Edison's baggage-car laboratory is probably neater than the original.

The profits from his newspaper sales allowed Al to buy more chemicals and equipment for his laboratory, which he'd moved from his parents' basement to a corner of the train's baggage car. However, the track was bumpy, and one day a bottle of phosphorus was pitched from his chemical rack. When the bottle broke, the phosphorus reacted with the air and burst into violent combustion. Al and the conductor barely managed to stop the fire. The Edison laboratory was no longer welcome on the Grand Trunk Railroad.

When he wasn't conducting experiments, Al continued to devote himself to reading. He was issued library card

Al Edison, Journalist

All his life, Edison would be involved with reporters and newspapers. For a brief time he actually printed his own newspaper, *The Weekly Herald*. He taught himself to set "sticks" of metal type and work a used press bolted to the floor of his train's baggage car. He gathered local stories about births and deaths, railroad news, and gossip. One bit of gossip prompted a large and angry man to throw Al into the St. Clair River. This ended his journalism career.

number 33 at the new Detroit Free Library. "My refuge was the [library]," he later wrote. "I started with the first book on the bottom shelf and went through the lot, one by one. I didn't read a few books. I read the library."

In the maze of tracks around a station, boxcars were often given a push to help them get where they needed to go. One day, Edison was waiting at the Mount Clemens station while his train changed cars. A lone boxcar rumbled toward the platform. Suddenly, Al threw down his papers and basket. There was a tiny child playing on the track in the path of the huge car! He leaped from the platform and carried the three-year-old to safety.

As it turned out, the little boy

"I didn't read a few books. I read the library."

–Thomas Edison

was the son of station telegrapher James Mackenzie. He'd wandered away while his father was receiving a message, and Mackenzie was sick with remorse. He wanted to repay the boy who'd saved his son. Remembering that young Al was fascinated by the telegraph and hung around the telegraph office whenever he could, the grateful father offered to teach him professional telegraphy. He could board with the Mackenzie family and have lessons every day.

Al was thrilled. He threw himself into the work of learning the new and exciting trade. After 10 days of lessons, he disappeared for several days, then returned with a complete working telegraph key of his own. He'd built the instrument himself from scrap metal, using knowledge he'd picked up by watching machinists and mechanics in their shops in Detroit.

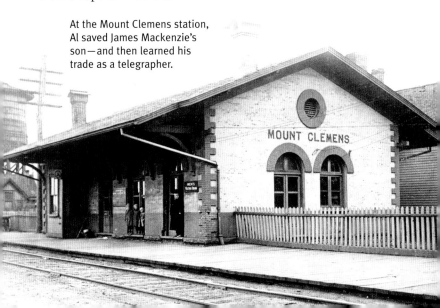

At the Mount Clemens station, Al saved James Mackenzie's son—and then learned his trade as a telegrapher.

Telegraphers tap outgoing messages, record incoming ones, then wait for the next piece of news.

Al and Mackenzie worked together for five months. Al learned well, quickly mastering the first tier of skills necessary to become a professional telegrapher: sending and receiving Morse code at 45 words per minute, and memorizing the shorthand abbreviations and operator's tricks that were part of telegraph language. He was ready, at 16, to be a "plug," a second-class telegrapher qualified for service almost anywhere along the line.

Telegraphy would end up shaping Al's future. Most of his patents emerged from his work with the new medium. Thomas Edison had found the current of his life—but he hadn't yet found his place.

A plug telegrapher could fit wherever there was an opening, and the Civil War created hundreds of jobs. Plugs were most often young men, shifting from job to job across the country, never staying long in one place. As part of the railroad system they could usually travel without a ticket, so a plug might leave his desk at any moment and board a train for San Francisco or Maine.

On the move, Edison began introducing himself as "Tom" rather than "Al." He traveled all over the Midwest and, when the Civil War ended, into the South. He was often far from home but never far from trouble.

He preferred the night shifts, from 7:00 PM to 7:00 AM, when little official work got in the way of reading and experimenting with batteries and new electrical ideas. It annoyed him that an operator was required to send a "six" ("• ————") every half hour, to show that he was alert. He rigged an old clock with a toothed wheel to send out the signal for him. One night, a suspicious supervisor replied to one of his sixes and discovered that Edison was not, in fact, alert. He was almost fired.

At Stratford, Ontario, a late signal allowed a train to rush past Edison's post toward another train. The alert engineers saw headlights and stopped in time to avoid disaster. Edison was summoned to Toronto, where the railroad's furious manager accused him of sleeping on the job and warned that failing an emergency signal was a prison offense. When the manager was distracted by visitors, Edison slipped out and, like his father before him, left Canada on the run.

Early telegraph machines functioned simply to make and break an electrical current, signifying a "dot" or "dash."

Tucked into corners, railroad telegraph offices weren't elegant workspaces.

Edison would be fired many times before his telegraph career was over. In Louisville, he spilled acid in the station's battery room. It ate through the floor, then through the manager's desk and his carpet below. Edison left for another dingy telegraph office down the line.

During these wandering years, Edison was always broke (his pay went toward books and experimental equipment). He wore shabby clothes and was usually uncombed and unshaven. Tom Edison was a "rube," lacking social manners, but he still read every book he could lay his hands on.

As he wandered, he tinkered, trying to improve the equipment he used. Several times, he rewired the offices in which he was working. When his supervisors found out, Edison had to replace his "improved" systems with standard wiring. Some of the lessons he was learning about the vast telegraph network were seeds for inventions that would develop later. A few developed more quickly out of necessity.

The stars of telegraphy were the operators who could copy down the long, rapidly keyed newspaper articles that were shared between cities. Edison was building up to the task but was still unsteady. He devised a particularly Edisonian invention: nothing entirely new, but something that gave existing equipment a new use. Recording telegraphs punched Morse code as dots and dashes into a long strip of paper from a reel. These strips could then be fed into another instrument to send the same dots and dashes. Edison recorded the rapidly sent message on one instrument, then looped the strip into a sending instrument set at a lower speed. Now that it was running at a slower pace, he could easily write down the code. The mechanism was simple and ingenious. But the station manager discovered that Tom was hanging up the strips while he read or experimented and not recording them until later, so he wouldn't allow anyone to use the device.

At another station Edison solved one of telegraphy's thorniest problems. Telegraph wires "leaked" current in many ways, so over long distances the signal faded. A message had to be sent to a relatively nearby station, not more than 40 miles (64 km) away, then re-sent by the operator there. Edison invented special weak-signal sensor coils to "hear" a dot or dash and activate a switch to automatically send it out using strong local batteries. In this way, a series of "relay" instruments could connect New Orleans with New York without the help of operators. This was a valuable invention. Sadly, the station manager and his nephew had been trying to solve the same problem. They were upset with Edison for finding a practical solution. He was fired again.

CURRENT

Current describes the movement of electrons through a conductor.

Edison was a small town boy but he had a sense of adventure borrowed from hundreds of books about heroic deeds. Moving from job to job as a plug, he was learning and trying out the flavors of life.

He discovered that he loved the theater, especially Shakespeare's *Othello* and *Richard III*. He saw famous actors who traveled from city to city playing one character on Monday, another on Wednesday. He even took part in some plays himself.

He also loved the German beer gardens where families could eat hearty food, drink beer, sing, and dance. Edison chewed tobacco and smoked cigars, but didn't drink more than an occasional beer. Many of his plug friends would leave their money with him before they went out on the town, trusting sober Tom to limit their spending.

From city to city, job to job, Edison's skill increased. In Cincinnati, he took over the night shift from friends who were out celebrating. Important news stories were coming in over the press wire, and he wrote them down as quickly and completely as he could. When the Western Union manager learned Edison had been successfully "taking press" for more than 12 hours, he promoted him to first-rate operator, assigned him to the Louisville press wire, and gave him a raise.

Unfortunately, Edison was slowly losing his hearing. This made him shy around women, but he still loved company. He listened as well as he could

PRESS WIRE

A press wire is a telegraph connection between newspapers.

to late-night talk, jokes, and songs. As a press operator, he was now part of the world of journalism. He especially liked newspaper writers. He saw how much influence the press had over public opinion, and learned how eager for stories every newsman was. These were lessons he would use to his advantage throughout his life.

Edison moved through the rough towns of the

A Parlor Trick Becomes a Workhorse

Electricity had been recognized for more than 100 years. Dr. Benjamin Franklin's experiments had established some of its basic properties, but no one had found a practical use for the curious phenomenon until the telegraph began flashing messages across the world. The effect of the technology on the imagination of the mid-19th century was powerful, symbolizing the possibility of progress and a bold new future for America.

former rebel states, still unstable during the postwar years. He said Memphis, Tennessee, was "wide open . . . demoralization reigned supreme. . . . The whole town was only 13 miles from Hell."

One dark night in Louisville, Kentucky, Edison walked toward his tiny, shared room carrying a bundle of old magazines he intended to read. An excitable policeman mistook him for a burglar carrying away his loot. The cop shouted at him to stop, but Edison, in his usual deep concentration, didn't pay much attention. When shots nicked dust off nearby bricks, he finally stopped. Luckily for Tom—and for the world—the policeman was a bad shot.

chapter **3**

Broke in Boston

Edison kept moving and learning. He developed his own style of plain, quick script to copy down messages and press stories—10 to 15 columns of news per day. He was so familiar with current events that he could often fill in the facts when interference along the wire or operator mistakes interrupted the flow of a story. He had become one of the best telegraphers on the broad web of "singing wires." His friend Milton Adams said that "as an operator he had no superior and very few equals." But telegraphy wasn't his real profession; Tom Edison was a professional inquirer.

In 1866, his curiosity led him to make a surprising decision: He quit his job to join a group of retired officers who had chartered a steamer to Brazil. But a riot in New Orleans held up the boat. While Edison waited, an old man told him, "If there was anything in a man the U.S. was the place to bring it out & that any man that left this country to better his condition was an ignorent [sic] damned fool. "

This chance meeting changed and saved his life—Tom's traveling companions went on to Brazil, where they died in a yellow-fever epidemic. Edison, meanwhile, returned to Louisville and his old job. He then returned to Port Huron and his family for a time. But something was different. Perhaps he recognized that behind his rash plans for the

Brazil journey was a need to find something really new. It was time for Edison to stop traveling and find his destiny in the United States.

As always, Tom Edison was drawn to science. At the time, the center of science and invention in America was

This fanciful image shows Edison telegraphing "across the world."

Boston, Massachusetts. Edison's friend Milton Adams arranged a job for him at the Western Union office there. Edison arrived in his usual state: broke, dressed in baggy, wrinkled clothes, looking like someone out of a potato patch.

The Boston operators thought they'd have some fun with the rube and asked the best operator in New York to send Edison a dispatch at his fastest speed. With a plug of tobacco in his cheek, Tom began to write out the dispatch without difficulty. Within a few minutes, he realized that it was a trick but he continued to take down the message calmly. When the New York operator was at his limit, slurring his words in code, Edison reached for his own telegraph key and replied, "Say, young man, change off and send with your other foot." The New York man laughed so hard he couldn't keep sending, and Tom became one of the boys.

In a used bookstore in Boston, Edison found a copy of *Experimental Researches in Electricity* by Michael Faraday, another self-taught scientist. Edison was awed. He read all night and hustled off to work without sleep. The clarity and simplicity of the book thrilled him. His brain churned with ideas!

He soon began to work on his experiments and inventions at the Charles Williams Jr. Machine Shop, among skillful machinists and mechanics. One of his colleagues was Charles Watson, who would later help Alexander Graham Bell develop the telephone.

During this time, Edison observed the ways telegraphy was influencing life beyond the railroads—for example, telegraphic fire alarms could now automatically alert fire stations when a blaze was detected. Technology was changing the world around him, and he wanted to be a part of it.

He also started investigating a new subject while he was in Boston: finance. Edison seldom knew how much money was in his pockets, but he was developing a sense of Big Money, the way

The handsome young Edison cut a dashing figure—when not playing pranks or chewing tobacco.

banks and businesses lent large sums to finance new ideas, inventions, industries. Perhaps one day he could harness some of that financial power.

Western Union was the giant among hundreds of smaller telegraph companies, and Edison was one of the best operators in the Boston office. But the work was largely routine: hours of waiting and a few minutes of intensity as he received or transmitted a news story. Edison passed the time reading and playing pranks. There was a jar of ice water in the office, with a tin dipper that often went missing. Edison put up a sign: "PLEASE RETURN DIPPER." Then he hooked the nail that held the dipper to a powerful battery. When an operator grasped the dipper, his arm and fist would cramp shut with the electric current. For weeks operators were reminded to return the dipper by their sore arms.

Later, Edison got a taste of his own medicine. He was trying a new wiring scheme and accidentally grabbed two battery cables. Current ran through both arms, clamping his fists shut. He couldn't let go! He had to stop the current.

Electricity in Miniature

In the late 19th century, electricity came in bottles: Glass lead-acid bottle batteries were just about the only source of electric power. They had to be refilled often with fresh acid and new metal plates. There were no generating plants, no transmission wires, and no "electric company." The source of electric current was messy, corrosive, smelly, dangerous, and, from a current perspective, small. Coaxing batteries to send a signal 60 miles (97 km) on poorly insulated wires was no easy task.

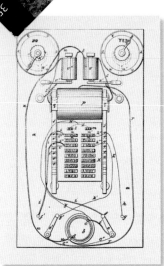

Edison's first patent, for an automatic vote counter, shows a complex mix of electrical principles and mechanics.

Shutting his eyes, he stepped back, toppling the wet-cell battery. Sulfuric acid spilled all over his face and chest—but the current was broken. He poured water over the burning acid. If his eyes hadn't been shut he would have been blinded. He later said, "I was a ghastly black and yellow. . . . It was two weeks before I could go out in the street again."

Meanwhile, Edison continued inventing and improving. Other inventors had created methods of sending messages two ways on the same wire at the same time. But Edison found a simpler and easier way. Investors took note, and businessmen became interested in financing his new ideas.

In 1868, Edison signed his first patent application, for an automatic vote recorder. He traveled to Washington, D.C., to demonstrate it to Congress. To record a vote, a congressman needed only to press a button on his desk when the roll was called. Votes were automatically counted, and each congressman received a printed record of his vote. The voting process would become quick and simple. The device was intelligent, well-developed, accurate, and ready to install.

PATENT

A patent is an official government record of a person's right to an invention.

Unfortunately, congressmen hated it. "Young man, if there is any invention on earth that we don't want down here it is this," they told him. As it turned out, they didn't want voting to be quick and efficient. Political parties and interest groups wanted voting to be slow and difficult so they had time to rush about the chamber making make last-minute deals. Brilliant or not, they didn't want new inventions changing their old devious ways.

Edison had invested months of time and bushels of money on a useless invention. Later, he said, "It was a lesson to me. There and then I made the vow I would never invent anything which was not wanted, or which was not necessary to the community at large."

Edison turned his attention from the world of politics to the world of business. The stock ticker had been developed in 1867 by E. A. Callahan as a kind of one-sided telegraphy for businessmen. A central office sent out continually updated quotes on the prices of publicly traded stocks and precious metals like gold and silver. Businesses subscribed to a special telegraph line and installed a receiving station in their offices, where a telegrapher would record the rise

Though impressive, the vote counter was ultimately an unwanted invention.

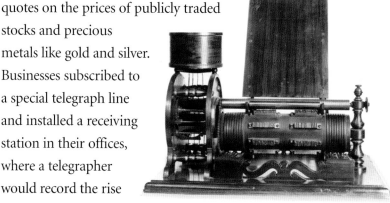

and fall of prices. Fortunes could be made over the hours of a day if businesses bought and sold shares wisely.

Edison started tinkering with stock tickers and saw that he could improve and simplify them. In January 1869, he applied for a second patent for his "improved stock ticker." This ticker

Edison's improved stock ticker printed out commodities prices on a paper ticker tape.

would print out a strip of paper, called "ticker tape," containing the abbreviated names of stocks or commodities, along with their prices. The tape could be printed without a professional telegrapher and could be read directly by businessmen.

With the backing of Boston financiers, Edison started a stock-reporting service using his ticker. The service gathered 30 subscribers in a short time, but patent disputes and disagreements arose when the invention was sold to a larger company. Before long, Tom Edison was broke again.

A failed businessman but a successful inventor, Edison had no desire to be an office telegrapher any more. He fooled around at the Western Union office with various pranks until he was about to be fired, then quit.

In June 1868, the *Journal of the Telegraph* carried an article, largely

> **COMMODITY**
>
> A commodity is a product such as wheat, steel, or gold that is traded by investors.

written by Edison, on a "mode of transmission both ways on a single wire . . . which is interesting, simple and ingenious." In January 1869 another notice appeared in a telegraphy journal: Thomas A. Edison, former operator, "would hereafter devote his full time to bringing out his inventions." He gave his work address as the Charles Williams Jr. Machine Shop, and announced the sale of his double transmitter at $400.

At the time, two-way telegraphy was a promising field. If messages could be sent in both directions by the same wire, it reduced the enormous amount of wire required to run long telegraph lines—many tons of it—by half. A test of Edison's system was arranged, and he once again had a very fine chance of becoming a wealthy young man.

The test was made on the lines of the Atlantic and Pacific Telegraph Company between Boston and New York. It was conducted over several days before the morning rush on the busy lines. But the telegrapher on the New York end didn't understand the equipment, and the trials failed.

In a way, Edison's shortcomings as a businessman gave him an advantage over other inventors: Money meant almost nothing to him. While others were desperate to turn a profit, Edison simply wanted to continue fooling around, learning new things, trying new ways to solve problems. Failure was nothing new to him. In fact, the failure of an idea or an invention had its value: It taught him what didn't work.

Still, a man needed money to finance his tinkering. So Edison decided to go where the money was: New York.

4

A Full-time Inventor

Edison bought a steamer ticket on borrowed money and arrived at the New York docks early in the morning without a cent in his pocket. He was 22 years old. He found an old friend who loaned him a dollar, and a good part of that went toward a big meal. Then he called at the Western Union office, but there were no job openings. So he took a long hike up Broad Street to the Gold Indicator Company, one of the telegraph stock-ticker services, where he met Franklin L. Pope.

Pope knew about Edison from articles the young man had published in the *Telegrapher,* a magazine for operators. There were no jobs available at Gold Indicator, but with night falling, Pope offered Edison a cot in the battery room where he could stay while he was looking for a job.

Founded by Dr. Samuel Laws, the Gold Indicator Company used a telegraph stock ticker similar to Edison's to report gold prices to a base of 300 clients. At the time, the price of gold was fluctuating rapidly, and speculators were following the changes moment by moment.

In the middle of a particularly busy day for the gold market, Laws's central transmitter stopped! Pope, who was the technical director, couldn't get it working again. Dozens of messengers from subscribers' offices arrived: The gold wire had gone dead—when would it be working again? Laws's business was close to collapse.

Edison was an easygoing fellow, never excitable. As messengers argued with Laws, and Pope opened and closed his mouth, unable to say a word, Edison looked at the sending device.

In a few minutes, the rumpled young man stepped up to Laws and suggested that he could probably fix the thing if he could get at it. "Fix it! Fix it!" Laws shouted. Edison took the cover off the transmitter and plucked out a spring that had fallen into the gears. In a short time, the gold prices were being sent out again. Edison had found himself a job.

Soon, Pope left to become an electrical consultant, and Edison took over as Laws's chief technical advisor. He improved the company so much that it was eventually bought out by Western Union. The new owners offered to keep him on as chief technician, but Edison had other ideas.

In late 1869, Edison formed a partnership with Pope and a silent partner, James Ashley, publisher of the *Telegraph*,

The Gold Standard

What is a dollar worth? In Edison's day, the value of the dollar was based on a set amount of gold. Since gold prices fluctuated rapidly, a shrewd investor watching the gold market could make a handsome profit by buying and selling gold when the dollar was high or low.

who contributed free advertising. Pope, Edison & Co. developed a simplified ticker that would print out the current prices of gold and silver and could be sold for less than the Edison-improved Laws ticker. When they had sold a few units, Western Union bought the patent for $15,000 to avoid competition. Edison was disappointed to receive only a third of the money, despite having conceived the idea and done all the development work. The rest went to Pope and Ashley. Edison continued his friendly relations with the men but dissolved the partnership. Big business was a dangerous place for a newcomer like Tom Edison.

Meanwhile, Western Union continued to control the telegraph industry, buying out competitors and purchasing the rights to any patent that would improve their service. Edison had patented several more telegraph devices when he solved a crucial problem.

Simple current interruptions or mechanical difficulties could make stock tickers misread the code transmitted on the line. Edison invented a unison correcting device that stopped all the tickers along a line and reset them at regular intervals. Both Edison and Western Union realized that the device was essential, and Western Union wanted to buy it. But how much should the inventor charge for the rights to his patent? He thought they might pay as much as $5,000 but was willing to settle for $3,000. When the president of Western Union asked him "How much?" Edison said something very smart: "Make me an offer."

Marshall Lefferts nodded and replied, "How does $40,000 strike you?"

Edison gulped and said that it struck him just fine. He walked out of Western Union headquarters with a check for $40,000. He'd never had so much money in his life. What should he do with it? He took it to the nearest bank and tried to cash it, but the teller handed it back to him. Edison stomped out of the bank and returned to the Western Union offices. Had they given him a bad check? Everyone was amused. Until now, Edison had always been paid in cash. He'd never cashed a check and didn't know his signature was needed on the back of the check to endorse it.

The bank cashed the endorsed check, and Edison stuffed away great stacks of $10 and $20 bills into the pockets of his cheap overcoat. He was a happy young man.

Night fell, and Edison boarded a train to Newark, New Jersey, where he'd been living with the Pope family. Suddenly, he realized that he was carrying a fortune in cash on a dimly lit train. He could be robbed! Had anyone seen him leave the bank with all this money? He was too frightened to sleep.

About 10 miles (16 km) outside of New York City, Newark, New Jersey, was a bustling city in its own right.

Edison returned to New York on the morning train wearing the same cash-stuffed overcoat and walked into General Leffert's office again. Where did wealthy men put their money? he asked. The general took him to a bank and helped him open an account. Edison had every reason to expect the account to remain flush with profits: In addition to payment for his patent rights, he had a contract to build 1,200 unison stock ticker–setting instruments for $500,000.

Edison busied himself with finding a shop, equipment, and employees. In the middle of his preparations, he received a telegram: His dear mother had died. He boarded a train for Port Huron immediately and arrived in time for the funeral. For many years, he was too upset to talk

Thomas Edison may be the man in the upper window, in this picture of his Newark factory.

about his mother. Much later he said, "The memory of her will always be a blessing to me."

As always, work was Edison's refuge, and he threw himself furiously into his manufacturing company to beat back the sadness of his mother's death. He began with 18 men and increased his workforce to 150. His factory was enlarged from a single rented floor to an entire building nearby, producing instruments day and night. He was seldom away from the factory; he was the foreman of both the day and the night shift.

Edison slept unpredictably. He'd always preferred working night shifts when no one would disturb his reading, but now he seemed to be up and about at all hours. He might nap on a workbench for an hour, drop exhausted on a cot and sleep for 12 hours, or go without sleep for three days. This was the strange pattern of his days and nights for most of his life.

It wasn't just Edison's sleeping schedule that was unusual. His approach to finance was haphazard and even primitive. For years he kept bills and statements on two hooks by his desk: money he owed, and money owed to him. As his factory made instruments and money came in, he paid as many of the bills as he could. Several bookkeepers tried to manage his accounts but threw up their hands and left. Business partnerships came and went. Edison was as jovial and pleasant as a man could be, but he would always be a loner. His background had trained him to be inventive, informed, skillful, hard-working, focused, and ambitious.

But very little in his history suggested he would ever be a businessman.

Edison was a jovial boss who put in longer hours than anyone else. He enjoyed the company of his "Boys," the male banter, and fun of the shop. He paid his workers well and demanded their best efforts. He attracted employees who understood his quirks, and they often stayed with him for many years. "Honest John" Kruesi was a German clockmaker who could create any machine Edison needed. John F. Ott was a mechanical prodigy who devised the workings of many Edison inventions. Charles Batchelor was an English draftsman who could develop Edison's basic but precise sketches into working drawings for new inventions.

As an up-and-coming industrialist, Edison now dressed marginally better, but he was still a social disaster. Around women, he was embarrassed, awkward, and hopeless. In Boston, he'd been asked to demonstrate Morse code to a class of

At the tender age of 16, Mary Stilwell went from employee to the boss's wife after a short, unexpected courtship.

young women and almost fainted. Yet he felt a young man should have a wife and family.

Mary Stilwell was barely 16 when Edison noticed her. One of his own factory employees, she was tall and buxom, with dark eyes and a sweetly turned mouth. At first, she found Edison's attention almost scary. He sometimes watched her work for minutes before speaking. By and by, with characteristic bluntness, he asked, "What do you think of me, little girl, do you like me?"

She stammered a moment before he added, "Don't be in a hurry about telling me. It doesn't matter much, unless you would like to marry me."

This statement resulted in more stammering.

He continued, "Oh, I mean it. . . . Think it over, talk to your mother about it, and let me know as soon as convenient; Tuesday, say."

When asked later how his deafness affected his courtship, Edison said that it gave him an excuse to get closer than other men might dare, and that "after things were going nicely, I found hearing unnecessary."

It was a very businesslike romance.

Tom and Mary Edison were married on Christmas Day in 1871. He was 24; she was still 16. After a wedding lunch he took her to the Newark home he'd bought

> *"What do you think of me, little girl, do you like me?"*
>
> –Thomas Edison,
> to his future bride

for her. Then, he left for the shop—there was a problem with the stock tickers he wanted to solve. Around midnight, his friend Murray saw the lab light and came in to interrupt him.

"Tom, what are you doing?" he asked.

"What time is it?" Edison replied.

"Midnight," Murray told him.

"Is that so? I must go home then, I was married today."

Mary was so overwhelmed by marriage (and probably by Tom) that she refused to go on a honeymoon to Niagara Falls unless her older sister, Alice, and Murray Adams went with them.

It was not a storybook marriage. Tom spent most of his time at the factory, sometimes staying there for days at a time. He would return so tired that he fell instantly asleep, still wearing his grimy lab clothes and shoes. Mary was not an intellectual companion, nor was she especially interested in science. In one of his lab notebooks Edison wrote, "My wife Popsy-Wopsy

Mary and Tom's children were (from left to right) William Leslie, Thomas Alva, Jr., and papa's favorite, Marion.

can't invent." For him, a wife seems to have been something like a sofa or an armchair: a comfortable addition any home should have. Mary liked to give fine parties, to which Tom never came. But she was sweet and loving, and thought her husband was a great man. She was also a great favorite among his workers, because she was once one of them and was always friendly.

The couple had three children. In a humorous play on Morse code, the first child, Marion (born in 1873), was nicknamed "Dot." The next, Thomas Alva Edison, Jr., (born in 1876) was nicknamed "Dash." The third was William Leslie Edison (born in 1878).

In the 13 years of their marriage Mary was, except for their children, largely alone. She was afraid of burglars at night and, her daughter Marion said, "often slept with a revolver under her pillow. One night my father forgot his key and not wishing to waken the whole place, climbed up the trellis on the porch roof to the bedroom window. Mother, thinking he was a burglar, almost shot him."

Tom Edison, Papa

It wasn't easy to be the child of a genius. Even when he was home, Edison was focused on inventions and had little time for his kids. He ate in silence. He wanted Tom, Jr., and Will to be inventors, like him, and brought them alarm clocks and other machines to take apart and fix. When Will found his toy train more interesting than broken clocks, Edison took the train away. He could be affectionate and playful, but he was mostly absent from his children's lives.

chapter 5

The Invention Factory

Edison's reputation as a young wonder was growing. It seemed that he could solve any problem. In the early 1870s, he was asked to improve on the British system of "automatic" telegraphy developed by George Little. Under Little's system, a user wrote a message on paper tape in the form of dot and dash perforations, then ran the tape rapidly between a metal wheel and a spring-loaded metal arm. The arm touched the wheel where the paper had been

Skillful drawings told Edison's Boys what to build. This one shows an automatic telegraph device.

punched out, making a brief electrical connection—and sending dots and dashes faster than human operators could achieve. At the receiving end of the system, a similar arm rode over a drum of chemically treated paper that changed color in response to electrical current, causing the dots and dashes to be printed out. In this way, a long message could be sent over wires in a short time, leaving the wires free for more messages.

In practice, however, the system was a disappointment. It worked well enough in the laboratory, at around 200 words a minute, but over long distances the dots and dashes often ran together. The receiving tape showed only a long line rather than distinct code.

Edison agreed to improve the Little system for a fee and a share in the profits. He tried the apparatus over long lines and diagnosed its difficulties. He researched the problem from an electrical, mechanical, and chemical perspective. Then he devised an easily manufactured message perforator. He designed new circuits that distinctly separated dots and dashes, even at high speeds. And he found a cheaper, better chemical to use in the expensive paper-treating solution.

The new telegraph machines received and printed messages on thin strips of paper that were fed through the mechanism.

This was one of many ideas Edison improved so thoroughly that it became a new invention. He drove the sending and receiving speed up to 3,000 words per minute. Even more astonishing, he created an elegant way to print out the message on tape in plain English letters rather than Morse code!

He'd become a bankable wizard. A telegraph expert said, "Edison's ingenuity inspired confidence, and wavering financiers stiffened up when it became known that he was [developing] the automatic [telegraph]."

Indeed, the British post office was interested in the Edison-Little automatic telegraph and requested a full-scale test. Though Marion, his first child, had just been born, Edison packed a trunk with equipment and, on April 29, 1873, boarded the steamship *Java* for a transatlantic trip to Great Britain.

At first, there were difficulties in Britain. Edison had to find stronger batteries and better wire than his hosts had provided for the tests. With the improved equipment, however, the trials of automatic telegraphy between Liverpool and London were successful, sending and receiving at over 1,000 words per minute.

The postal authorities then asked if the system would work over their long underwater cables. Edison thought it should. Twenty-two hundred miles (3,540 km) of submarine cable, ready to be laid between Gibralter and Brazil, was available for testing.

The armored, rubber-clad cable was coiled underwater at Greenwich. Edison sent a single dot at one end and expected a single dot to appear at the other. But the system's electric arm printed a 27-foot (8-m) line on the special paper instead. Edison couldn't make it work!

His failure to send automatic messages along the submarine cable pointed to a lapse in cable technology of the time. The enormous length of the wire together with poor insulation lengthened the signal. Another probable issue, which Edison may not have understood, was induction: When current passes through a wire, it creates

Submarine telegraph cable, used to take messages across the Atlantic, is coiled in a cable-laying ship.

a surrounding magnetic field that can "induce" current to flow in nearby wires. The long trip through the cable's closely coiled spiral of parallel wires lengthened the short signal into a long signal, like an echo chamber lengthens a noise. Eventually, when cable was laid beneath the Atlantic, the system worked well.

After six weeks, Tom Edison returned to New Jersey. The trip had been fruitless. The post office had chosen another system. Then, when he returned to his factory, his mood went from bad to worse: A red flag was nailed to his shop door, indicating that the county sheriff was about to close it down and sell the equipment for unpaid taxes.

Edison's quaint but unrealistic financial methods had nearly ruined his business. Mary helped a little, borrowing enough money from a friend to delay the foreclosure. Unfortunately, the U.S. economy was suffering a downturn at the time. Money men who had been eager to invest in new schemes a year before wouldn't see him now. A more trusting and economically educated man might have kept reliable partners who would help him reshape his finances. But Edison was a loner. For him there was only one solution: Try harder, work longer hours, and create more inventions.

One of the inventions Edison patented during this time was the "electric pen," the first office-based product to reproduce business documents in large quantities.

At the top of the pen was a tiny electric motor, about the size of a plum, connected to a pair of wet-cell batteries by a wire. When a switch was flipped, the motor drove a long needle up and down inside the pen. A "master" document was created using special waxed paper: As the user wrote, the rapidly pecking needle made a series of tiny holes in the paper, tracing out each letter and word. Then the paper was pressed down over a blank sheet, a gel-like ink was pushed across it with a rubber squeegee, and the document was printed as the ink squeezed through the holes. As many as 5,000 copies could be printed from a single master document.

There were several extraordinary features of this "pen." It was probably the first electric appliance, the first real power tool, and one of the first consumer electric devices. The invention was developed, improved, and then sold to a Chicago company, A. B. Dick, as the Edison Mimeograph. The mimeograph was used around the world for 100 years, until Xerox made optical copying practical. The alcohol smell of the mimeograph machine is still a powerful memory

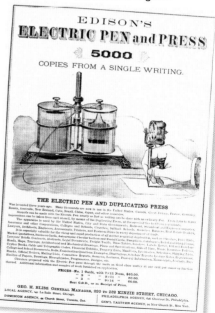

Edison's electric pen is advertised in this flyer, which shows it being used to write a note. Its lead-acid batteries are encased in glass.

EDISON'S
ELECTRIC PEN and PRESS
5000
COPIES FROM A SINGLE WRITING.

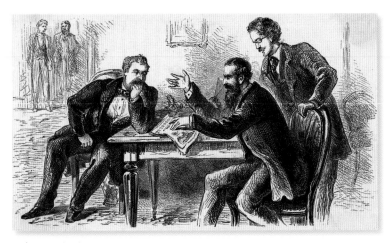

Jay Gould (left) famously plots to manipulate the gold market in 1869.

for anyone who worked in an office before 1970.

Despite the success of the electric pen, telegraphy was still the core of Edison's work. He devoted his deepest attentions to an idea he and many other inventors had pursued for years: sending simultaneous messages on the same wire.

Western Union made a loose agreement to back Edison's work on multiple messaging, giving him a place to work at their headquarters, assigning technicians to him, and providing him with open telegraph wires. The fancy workroom didn't excite Edison. It had marble-tiled floors, "which, by-the-way, was a very hard kind of floor to sleep on," he later noted.

POLARITY

Polarity describes opposite qualities of electric charge: positive or negative.

Nevertheless, Edison's work was a success. He found two ways to differentiate distinct signals on a wire: switching the polarity and varying the voltage strength. By combining the two

VOLTAGE

Voltage measures the force of an electrical current.

methods, Edison could send two messages in each direction—four messages in all—simultaneously on a single wire. He called his system the quadruplex.

Since the quadruplex would multiply message traffic and reduce the need for additional lines, it was potentially an enormous profit builder. But Western Union, resistant to the change, paid Edison a token sum that didn't even cover the cost of the 20 quadruplex instruments he had manufactured for the tests.

Meanwhile, a financial war was simmering. Jay Gould, a notorious railroad baron, was trying to seize control of Western Union, using patents and stock deals to gain power. Thomas Eckert was a Western Union official who was about to defect to Gould's Atlantic and Pacific Telegraph. Eckert suggested to Edison that Gould would pay him much more than Western Union, and more quickly. Edison and Eckert met Gould at his mansion, sneaking in through the servants' entrance to

Automatic Telegraphy

Though rejected by the British post office, the Edison-Little system of sending rapid messages by tape was up and running in the United States by 1875—and Gould's investment in Edison began paying off. One reporter wrote, "This system enabled the Atlantic & Pacific company to handle a much larger business during 1875 and 1876 than it could otherwise have done with its limited number of wires in their then condition." It wasn't the perfect solution to the technological limitations of the day, but it was helping move information faster and easier than ever before.

avoid being seen. Gould offered $30,000 as a first payment for the rights to the quadruplex. Edison jumped at the offer.

Gould and Edison were completely different characters. Edison was driven by his fascination with the way things worked, loved stories and jokes, and was doggedly persistent in solving problems. The humorless Gould, on the other hand, was interested solely in money, and once he made his bundle from a project would drop it like a hot potato. Edison should have remembered a very old saying: "He who sups with the devil should have a long spoon."

By this time, Edison had three or four workshops, and ideas were bubbling in all of them. Dozens of projects were going on at any given moment. Edison had an unusual way of refreshing himself, often taking a "vacation" from one project to work on another.

One project that engaged his attention was a contraption invented by Christopher A. Sholes. This device consisted of a box of wood displaying rows of buttons attached to long arms inside. Each arm was tipped with a sharply formed metal letter. When a button was pressed, the corresponding letter would fly up and strike a sheet of paper wound around a rubber roller. An inked ribbon held between the letter-arm and the roller made the imprint of the

> *"Mr. Gould was not one to breed warm friendships or even acquaintanceships."*
>
> –T.G. Sherman, Gould's legal advisor

letter on the paper. This was the first typewriter. For a time, the device was called a "literary piano," but its early music was sour. The line of letters on the paper wasn't neat and regular. Edison worked on the mechanics of the typewriter with his skilled machinists, assured by his confident intimacy with instruments of all kinds. In a few months, he had

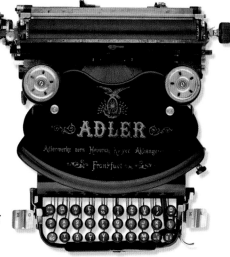

"Literary piano" was one name for the early typewriter. The keyboard is arranged similarly to a modern computer's keys.

upgraded Sholes's invention to a reliable office tool. It was manufactured and sold as the Remington typewriter, and the typewriter became a standard of business communication for more than century.

Tom Edison is part of our everyday lives in dozens of ways; the legacy of the typewriter is one of them. Although actual typewriters have now fallen out of use, the modern computer keyboard is nearly identical to a typewriter's. Its letters are arranged in the same sequence, the shift from lowercase to capital letters is achieved the same way, and the act of typing a message on a computer uses the very same finger and hand movements that Sholes and Edison explored.

chapter **6**

Menlo Park

E dison felt he would be able to concentrate better and spend less money if he lived and worked in the country. Thanks to his recent successes, he had some money, but he knew that it would be gone in no time. Why not spend it on a workshop specially built for invention?

He was too busy with new discoveries and ideas to scout for locations, so he invited his father, Sam, to scour the countryside for a likely spot. For his "Tommy," Sam found a sleepy little hamlet about 25 miles (40 km) southwest of New York City, a short train ride from the hubbub. At the time, Menlo Park, New Jersey, had only seven houses and a train station, but it was perfect for Edison's purposes. He bought a tract of land, and Sam went to work as superintendent, overseeing the construction of a two-floor wooden building, 100 feet (30 m) long by 30 feet (9 m) wide. A handsome picket fence kept out cows and pigs.

The ground floor held Edison's mechanical equipment, and the second floor became his testing laboratory. In a short time there was also a machine shop, carpentry shop, business office, library, and several small outbuildings. Tom bought a nearby farmhouse for Mary and his children.

The move turned out to be a test of loyalty. Thirteen of Tom's "Boys" moved to the country with him. Most of them moved into Sarah Jordan's boarding house on Christie Street (the only street in the village). Mrs. Jordan was a good feeder, famous for her pies, and the Boys settled in happily. Many would work for Edison most of their lives, making a good salary, but sacrificing their family lives to Edison's strange night-and-day schedule. John Ott, who worked beside Edison for 50 years, said, "Edison made your work interesting. He made me feel that I was making something with him. I wasn't just a workman."

Work was Edison's religion, and Menlo Park became his temple. He wanted to leave the business problems of manufacturing to others and devote himself entirely to discoveries. In fact, by moving to the new location, Edison had created his greatest and most lasting invention: the research laboratory. Menlo Park was the ancestor of Bell Labs, Los Alamos,

This Menlo Park lab, an original Edison building, was moved to Henry Ford's museum village in Michigan.

Jet Propulsion Laboratory, and other establishments
dedicated to working out scientific problems, uncovering
new knowledge, and producing new tools.

It was not an easy life. Menlo Park had a tiny saloon
with a single pool table. There was no social life beyond the
almost monastic order of Edison's workers. But there was a
passionate spirit that could drive the Boys (many of whom
were older than their 30-year-old boss) to engage in 60-hour
marathons of work to solve a problem.

It was a brotherhood and it had its rituals. Midnight
suppers were the favorite time for most,

Chemicals and a pipe organ
share an upstairs room
above the metal shops at
the Menlo Park labs.

Most of the Menlo Park compound can be seen in this aerial sketch of the buildings on a snowy day.

when someone fetched food, hot coffee, and pie from the boarding house. During these breaks from work, someone would play the big organ set up on the second floor, and some of the Boys played guitars. Stories were told, poems were recited, songs were sung, clog dances were stepped out. New York reporters who had missed the last train to the city joined in and left in the morning, amazed at the "laboratory that never sleeps."

Tom Edison used all his knowledge of reporters and newspapers to slyly court the attention of the press. He was always good for a story, or even for a handsome quote. "Genius is one percent inspiration and ninety-nine percent perspiration," he famously said. Edison used the press to publicize his work and his inventions, and to wage a private battle with the "theoretical scientists" and academics who looked down on practical engineers and inventors like Edison, Alexander Graham Bell, Christopher Sholes, or anyone with a practical goal.

For Edison, the only goal was hardware that worked—and that brought in money to finance his New Jersey country brotherhood.

chapter 7
His Favorite Invention

The telegraph was growing up. Once limited to sending dots and dashes, it was now learning to do tricks. It could transmit numbers and letters. In 1875, inventor Elisha Gray was able to transmit 16 different musical notes on a device he called the telephone.

Parallel invention is an odd reality in science. Over and over in scientific history, multiple researchers have worked on the same problem simultaneously. In 1876, several clever people were asking the telegraph to "speak." Elisha Gray and

Alexander Graham Bell was an educator of the deaf, an inventor, and one of Edison's professional rivals.

Alexander Graham Bell filed papers at the patent office for a method of transmitting human speech over telegraph lines within hours on the same day. Ultimately, Bell was awarded the patent, one of the most valuable in history.

Bell's invention was a hit at the 1876 Centennial Exposition in Philadelphia—but it was still a crude instrument. The "magnetotelephone" used sound waves to generate a weak, variable current. Its maximum range was about two miles (3 km), and the caller had to shout his sentences two or three times to be understood. Western Union president William Orton realized the value of the telephone, and asked Edison to work on improving the concept. It was a difficult task: Bell's device made only a faint sound, and Edison's hearing had gotten worse.

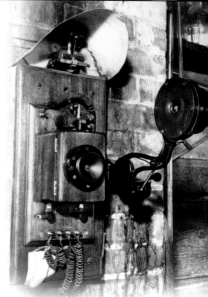

Edison's separate transmitter and receiver set the pattern used in telephones to this day.

The biggest challenge was converting sound waves to strong electrical signals. Edison had noticed that carbon granules transmitted electricity at different rates according to the pressure applied. Could sound waves from the human voice be used to compress the carbon? He tried a number of arrangements until he found that a simple carbon button between plates of steel could convert sound into electrical waves. He had invented the microphone.

Early telephones had used the same device to transmit and receive signals. Edison soon realized that separating the transmitter and receiver would make the telephone work better. He also added an induction coil to strengthen the signal

CARBON

Carbon is a chemical element sometimes seen as the black product of combustion, as in charcoal.

for long-range use. In a test of Edison's improved telephone between Philadelphia and New York, a distance of 107 miles (172 km), voices came through loud and clear.

Edison was at a disadvantage in his telephone research because he couldn't hear his results well. He counted on others to detect improvements. But he thought about sound more than most people. The microphone had shown him that sound could "do work." He even made a mechanical paper doll for his daughter, Dot. When she shouted down a funnel, the sound waves made the little doll saw a paper log.

At this same time, Edison was investigating ways to use sound's energy to make a permanent record of what was said, something on which businesses could depend, a "file copy." In June 1877 he was working on a kind of graphic telephone transcript using a strip of wax paper. A stylus connected to a diaphragm made scratches in the wax. When he pulled the paper out to change it, the scratches made a

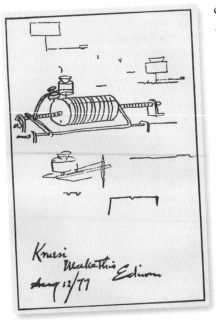

"Make this," was Edison's simple, groundbreaking order to Honest John Kruesi.

faint, almost musical sound, like human voices speaking in the next room. If random dots and dashes could sound like human voices, could the sound

DIAPHRAGM

A diaphragm is a light disk that vibrates in response to sound waves.

waves of a human voice be captured and played back?

Due to his work on the telephone, diaphragms were on Edison's mind. He attached another strip of wax paper and shouted, shouted "Halloo!" He and his assistant Charles Batchelor (who had excellent hearing) then pulled the strip out. A sound was heard. It might have been "Halloo!" It was close enough to investigate further.

Edison didn't even know what he expected. Could a machine record telephone conversations? Perhaps it could be used as a relay to send voice communication over longer lines? What kind of machine would record and play back sound?

In November, Edison gave a sketch of a possible machine to Honest John Kruesi, who thought the idea was crazy. But Edison was determined to give it a try. Kruesi built a brass cylinder that held a sheet of tinfoil wrapped around it. The cylinder was turned with a handle and was attached to a diaphragm and blunt pin that rode along the tinfoil as the cylinder was turned. Edison's workers bet "the Old Man" several cigars that it wouldn't work. Even Edison didn't believe it would do much.

Edison fixed the tinfoil to the cylinder, swung the diaphragm and pin into place, and turned the handle, shouting into a cup around the diaphragm:

Edison's original hand-cranked phonograph is shown here without its single-use foil recording surface.

"Mary had a little lamb, its fleece was white as snow. And everywhere that Mary went, the lamb was sure to go."

He swung off the pin, rewound the cylinder back to its starting place, and replaced the diaphragm with a larger version attached to a sound horn. Putting the pin in place again, he turned the handle. Edison's recorded voice shouted the nursery rhyme out of the strange machine.

Edison later said, "I was never so taken aback in all my life. Everybody was astonished. I was always afraid of things that worked the first time." After a long period of silence, the Boys broke into excited chatter. They worked (and played) all night with the new invention. The human voice had been recorded for the first time.

On December 7, 1877, Tom Edison walked into the offices of *Scientific American* in New York with a package. He unwrapped it and described what it was about to do. He recorded his voice, and played it back.

At first, no one believed it. It was a ventriloquist's trick! Then, people came from all over the building until no more could enter the room. The next issue of *Scientific American* reported, "The machine began by politely inquiring as to our health, asked how we liked the phonograph, informed us that it was very well, and bid us a cordial good night."

Public clamor was unbelievable. No one—certainly not Edison—could have predicted the stir made by this small device. It was a marvel. It was miraculous: the human voice recorded!

Responding to buzz about the phonograph, Alan Cumming from the *New York Sun* visited Menlo Park to write a profile of Edison. He described the inventor's earthy charm, unassuming appearance, and country boy's modesty, as well as his zeal in describing inventions yet to come. Edison wasn't an airy academic or a distant scientist, but a plainspoken man who enjoyed a cigar and a joke. He wasn't just a learner but was also a "doer," a grown-up boy playing with particularly wonderful toys and excited by his ability to make things happen. He was an American original.

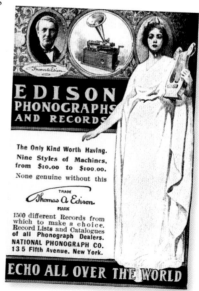

This 1901 advertisement shows a picture of the inventor and his favorite invention.

Before the phonograph, Edison had created profitable and useful inventions for telegraphy, but he wasn't well-known beyond a few electricians, telegraph plugs, and financiers (and a few

An unusually somber Edison sits beside his improved 1878 phonograph.

sheriffs who had almost closed him down). Soon, however, Edison's workshop was crowded with reporters. Fame had arrived at Menlo Park.

The phonograph caught the public's imagination like nothing else. It was unexpected and almost unbelievable. It simply arrived in its glory and was celebrated by every newspaper and magazine.

The railroad brought crowds of sightseers to sleepy little Menlo Park. It was a curious destination. The place was small and looked more like a long Baptist church than a temple of science. It manufactured nothing, yet its workers were intensely busy creating real magic. It was like no other place in the world. The *New York Daily Graphic* gave Edison a name—"the Wizard of Menlo Park"—and it stuck.

It wasn't only the public who praised the magic of the phonograph, but also scientists, statesmen, writers, and academics. And praise came not just from America but from across the Atlantic, as well. Edison was requested to make the phonograph talk for the Smithsonian Institution, for members of Congress, and even for President Rutherford B. Hayes, who was enchanted.

The phonograph craze was powerful—and somewhat hard to understand from a modern perspective. Perhaps the invention represented the bright new mechanized world, the marriage of science and technology. For a "rube," Edison was masterful in the way he dramatized the phonograph for the press. This invention, almost accidental, established Edison as a genuine celebrity.

It was a magnificent invention, but so far it had no real purpose. Edison and his Boys improved the design, but it was still difficult to use, not yet a consumer product. Phonographs were leased to "exhibitors" who gave shows in museums, storefronts, and churches. For several years the device was a glittering wonder. But when nearly everyone in the United States had seen and heard an exhibition, the novelty was gone, and the wonder seemed to have no future.

Nevertheless, the phonograph was Edison's favorite creation, and he still had hopes for it. "Yes . . . this is my baby, and I expect it to grow up and be a big feller and support me in my old age," he said. He considered making further improvements and mass-producing prerecorded cylinders, but realized that this was a new kind of invention; it would require an entire support structure dedicated to recording, manufacturing, reproducing, and marketing. At the moment,

Edison was too giddy with the excitement of invention to think about slogging through all those practicalities.

And so Tom Edison set aside his favorite invention, now merely a scientific curiosity, for 10 years.

The media blitz had exhausted Edison. He needed a vacation from fame. In July 1878, he was invited by Professor George F. Barker to join a group of astronomers for a viewing of a total eclipse of the sun from the Rocky

Edison's Hopes For the Phonograph

In June 1878, Edison wrote a magazine article suggesting possible uses for his invention. Many are realities today:

1. Letter writing, and all kinds of dictation without the aid of a stenographer.

2. Phonographic books, which will speak to blind people without effort on their part.

3. The teaching of elocution.

4. Music—The phonograph will undoubtedly be liberally devoted to music.

5. The family record; preserving the sayings, the voices, and the last words of the dying members of the family, as of great men.

6. Music boxes, toys, etc.—A doll which may speak, sing, cry or laugh may be promised our children for the Christmas holidays ensuing.

7. Clocks, that should announce in speech the hour of the day, call you to lunch, send your lover home at ten, etc.

8. The preservation of language by reproduction of our Washingtons, our Lincolns, our Gladstones.

9. Educational purposes; such as preserving the instructions of a teacher so that the pupil can refer to them at any moment; or learn spelling lessons.

10. The perfection or advancement of the telephone's art by the phonograph, making that instrument an auxiliary in the transmission of permanent records.

Mountains. Edison wanted to use the trip to try out yet another new invention. The "tasimeter" was a spin-off of his carbon-button microphone that could measure extremely small variations in heat. He thought he could attach

"This is my baby, and I expect it to grow up and be a big feller and support me in my old age."

–Edison, speaking about the phonograph

a tasimeter to a telescope to measure the temperature of the sun's corona. It didn't work. Nevertheless, Tom wasn't dismayed, because he'd accomplished something important. He said, "I can never find the thing that does work best until I know everything that don't do it."

With a note from Jay Gould, one of the principals of the Union Pacific Railroad, Edison was allowed to sit anywhere he wanted on the train down out of the Rockies. For almost three days he occupied the grand perch of his choosing: 10 yards (9 m) ahead of the engineer, on the cowcatcher— a frame on the front of the locomotive, meant for clearing track debris. He was out in the open, with an almost unlimited view of the path ahead.

Edison's trip to the Rockies refreshed him. It also presented him with a serious challenge. In the evenings during the trip, Professor Barker had urged Edison to look into the possibility of a new frontier of invention: practical electric lighting.

chapter **8**

Let There Be Light!

In Edison's time, the night was lit by fire. Before 1870, the darkness after the sunset was broken only by candles, oil, or gas. The petroleum came mainly from recently drilled wells in Pennsylvania, and was refined into kerosene for use in wick lamps.

Glass lamps, once the standard in home lighting, featured brass wickholders and a chamber for holding kerosene or other fuel.

"Town gas," made by heating coal, was piped to subscribers. Gas lamps were expensive, however, and were installed only on some city streets and in a few wealthy homes.

The success of telegraphy suggested there might be other uses for electricity. Could it be used to make light? At the Centennial Exposition in 1876, Moses Farmer displayed an arc light: Electricity from a steam dynamo made a spark (or "arc") between two carbon rods to produce an eerily bright light. Two years later, Russian engineer Pavel Yablochkov was lighting the streets of Paris with carbon arc lights. The lamps were dazzling but required massive amounts of current, burned with an unpleasant glare, and their carbon rods lasted only about 200 hours.

Another method of making electric light was incandescence. Electricity flowing through a filament (a thin strip made of various materials) gave out a glow. But a current that was strong enough to produce a glow destroyed filaments in a few seconds. Some inventors tried protecting their filaments in a vacuum within a glass globe. British inventor Joseph Swan had pursued this idea for many years. Canadian inventors Henry Woodward and Mathew Evans used a nitrogen-filled glass bulb and carbon rods. None of their lamps gave much light or lasted long.

In 1878, Edison visited the Moses Farmer factory, which made dynamos and arc lamps. He had been lukewarm about a light project, but when he saw the 500-candlepower lights and the 8-horsepower dynamo, something in him blazed up. He strode back and forth among the machines

The Dynamo

A dynamo is a tool for converting mechanical motion (from a waterwheel, windmill, or steam engine) into electric current. The mechanical energy turns coils of wire within a magnetic field. As the coils rotate through the changing push and pull of the magnet's forces, electrons in the coils are induced to flow through the wire, resulting in an electric current that can be used to power machines.

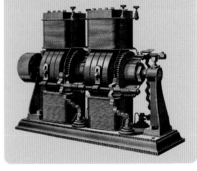

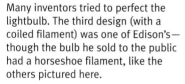

Many inventors tried to perfect the lightbulb. The third design (with a coiled filament) was one of Edison's—though the bulb he sold to the public had a horseshoe filament, like the others pictured here.

and instruments. He threw himself on a workbench and filled pages of his notebook with calculations and notes. He shook the hand of Wallace's partner and said happily, "I believe I can beat you making the electric light. I do not think you are working in the right direction."

Edison had a great start: He knew what his light shouldn't be. Arc light was too bright, too searing. Instead of a few flaring suns, homes needed many gentle moons giving more personal, controllable light. Edison was certain that the smaller-scale, lower-current, and more difficult method of incandescence would do the trick.

Edison was enthused. On the trip back to Menlo Park, he made a rash promise to a reporter. Within six weeks, he would invent a practical electric light, throw up poles, and install lights in Menlo Park houses for a grand exhibition. At the time he didn't have the faintest idea how he could do it.

Back at the shop he read every book he could find

"I start where the last man left off."

–Thomas Edison

about electric lights. He looked at every other inventor's ideas, learning from their mistakes and their successes. He and the Boys began hundreds of experiments. A carbon filament was the most obvious choice, but they couldn't make it last for more than eight minutes.

Soon, Edison faced the fact that it would be a long, hard trip to success. That meant more assistants, and more money. He'd developed a platinum filament that was impressive, but he knew that this precious metal was much too expensive to market. He needed press coverage to bring in investors, so he demonstrated a platinum filament bulb for the New York papers. It gave a lovely light. The reporters were amazed, worshipful. They wrote it up as a wonder that just needed "a few bugs ironed out." The truth was that Edison knew he hadn't found the right filament.

A syndicate of investors was impressed enough to fund his work, and in October 1878, Edison formed the Edison Electric Light Company. Unfortunately, the money ran out at the end of the year. Edison assured his backers that success was near, so they put up more development money, and the work went on for 10 more months. Edison learned how to create a better vacuum inside the glass globe, but the right filament continued to elude Edison and the Boys.

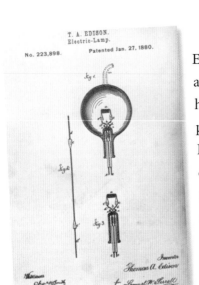

T. A. EDISON.
Electric-Lamp.
No. 223,898. Patented Jan. 27, 1880.

The patent drawing of Edison's lightbulb shows how the bulb connects to a power source (top) and its coiled filament (bottom).

The platinum filament Edison had shown the press was a precious metal that would have been too expensive to produce in mass quantities. He tried cotton, fishing line, cardboard, and paper. He tried a series of metals, including iridium, titanium, and zirconium. He wanted to try tungsten (which is what most modern filaments are made of), but it required complex equipment the lab didn't have.

On October 21, 1879, Edison kneaded cotton sewing thread in finely ground lampblack (a type of soot). He baked the thread, then mounted it in a vacuum-filled glass globe. When the battery was attached, the light glowed. The glow wasn't dramatic at first. So many filaments had failed after a few minutes. But the new light kept burning. All night, all the next day. The Boys sat and watched it for hours, waiting for it to fail.

In the end, the light burned for over a day. Edison said, "If it will burn that number of hours now, I know I can make it burn a hundred!" He turned up the voltage bit by bit until he found the filament's limits. There was a bright flash and a pop. Only then did the first practical incandescent electric lightbulb burn out.

Edison's vision was vast. The lightbulb itself meant nothing without a system to support it. That meant a constant source of current from big dynamos and a network of wires to deliver electricity. What he envisioned was the world's first electric company: He would find a way to measure electricity so that subscribers would pay for it "by the pound."

The Filament

Carbonized thread worked well as a filament, but Edison still wasn't satisfied. He continued testing fibers of every kind for his new lightbulb: More than 6,000 filaments made of every vegetable, metal, and mineral the Boys could find. He finally settled on carbonized bamboo as the most satisfactory filament.

Producing that electricity was still a tricky process; existing dynamos were inefficient and expensive to build. So Edison assembled a team of college-trained electrical engineers to began to examining ways to improve the technology. The team set out to consider every type of dynamo for its virtues and drawbacks. Their improved dynamo would have to produce more current than any previous system, and run all day and all night, year-round.

This replica of Edison's first practical lightbulb was made for the 50th anniversary of its invention by the inventor himself.

Edison's team had to manufacture not just the bulbs, but also the hardware to mount them: sockets, insulated wire, connectors, switches—none of it existed yet! He also had to design an overall method of wiring districts, streets, and houses. As a practical concern, every lightbulb had to be independent, allowing people to turn a single lamp on and off without affecting other bulbs. Fire was always in mind, so safety was a major concern.

Edison also struggled with another major problem: How could electricity turn a profit during daylight hours, when the lights weren't needed? He soon threw himself into inventing electric motors, pumps, and even an electric railroad train. Three miles of electric tracks were laid on insulated ties around Menlo Park, a place the newspapers now called "the invention factory." Perhaps this was the reason Edison was so casual about predicting the success of incandescent light: The lightbulb itself was only a small part of the vision.

The electric system would work best best in a densely populated urban area. This way, electric wires could be short, close to the dynamo, and serve the maximum number of people. Downtown Manhattan would be perfect. This area also had the advantage of being close to the financial backers who would fund even larger projects.

Unfortunately, backers balked at the enormous project. A financial friend suggested that Edison offer a demonstration by electrifying Menlo Park to win them over. Soon, light poles were raised, the electric wires were laid in buried pipes, and lightbulbs were manufactured in great numbers. On New Year's Eve 1879, Tom Edison at last made his boast reality. Menlo Park was transformed to a magical nighttime vision with more than 400 electric bulbs lighting streets, houses, and the lab itself. The Pennsylvania Railroad scheduled special trains so New Yorkers could see the spectacle.

The press and the public were enchanted. They were especially delighted by the fact that the lights could be turned on and off. "No Admission" signs on the dynamo room didn't keep out several men, whose pocket watches stopped cold, magnetized by the strong electric field. Eight lightbulbs were stolen, and an electrician in the pay of a gas-lighting company tried to kill the entire show by short-circuiting the supply wires. Because Edison had isolated sections of wiring with fuses, only four lightbulbs blew out. (The saboteur was seized and thrown out of the lab by some of the Boys.) There were so many visitors that the Boys feared the lab's floor might cave in! Over the course of a single night, and the following day,

On New Year's Eve, 1879, visitors to Menlo Park were enchanted by "the invention factory."

"Nothing that's good works by itself, just to please you. You've got to make [it] work."

–Thomas Edison

more than 3,000 people shattered Menlo Park's quiet order.

Edison was a showman but he was also shy. He put up with all the exposure he could and then hid. The *New York Tribune* reported, "Edison is one of the most retiring of men, detesting all pomp and show, resembling the ladies in his desire to get away into the forest of solitude." Menlo Park was closed to visitors on January 2.

One reason for Edison's discomfort was that the hard work of building the electric system lay ahead. Indeed, two years of frantic labor lay before him. So far, his work on light had already cost him more time and energy than any other project. He was practically obsessed, working at all hours without a pause. One journal commented, "We hope that he will not drive on at this Herculean task, until, some day, despite . . . his extraordinary powers of endurance, he has sacrificed his health and broken down, on his work."

At the heart of the system were the machines that produced electricity. At the time, electric dynamos were still mysterious contraptions. Scientific theory about how they worked was sketchy and unreliable. The prevailing wisdom held that no dynamo could achieve more than 50 percent efficiency. The results of experiments were hazy, because there were no instruments to measure some of the most basic electrical properties, such as electrical force (voltage) and flow (amperage). Edison and the Boys were performing pioneering research in electrical theory, leaving the "theoretical scientists" in their wake.

Edison hated the way that the leather belts that connected steam engines to tools (and to his dynamos) wasted energy. He went through several engines before he found one he could connect to his dynamo with a steel shaft, instead.

The dynamo Edison eventually developed was a big iron block with two thick cylinders. The Boys called it the "Long-Legged Mary Ann," but the name was later changed

Edison's early dynamo, nicknamed the "Long-Waisted Mary Ann," was revolutionary in its form and its high efficiency.

to the "Long-Waisted Mary Ann," since it was considered to be in poor taste to refer to a woman's legs. It tested out at 90 percent efficiency.

Edison also started a lightbulb factory. One of his suppliers began to make sockets and hardware, and Edison bought two adjacent buildings on Pearl Street in lower Manhattan and refit their interiors with iron beams to prepare for his oversize dynamos. The system was coming together.

chapter **9**

The Electric Company

Edison's electric company was not the first one in New York City. In 1880, the Brush Electric Company supplied and powered arc lights over a section of Broadway as a demonstration. Brush moved on to install arc lights on other New York streets and even in a few offices. However, the quality of arc light was unpleasant, and the lights were also dangerous. They started many fires, and several people were electrocuted while working on them.

The United States Electric Lighting

Edison personally oversees workers laying his cable underground.

Company produced an incandescent lightbulb designed by the inventor Hiram Maxim, who later invented the machine gun. Instead of Edison's horseshoe-shaped filament, it had an M-shaped (for Maxim) light source. It infringed on Edison's patent, but Edison was so confident that his product was better, he didn't bother to sue. In the late

1870s, Maxim installed and powered 150 M-bulbs in the headquarters of an insurance company—the first electric lights to be installed in a New York City building.

However, none of these early pioneers in the world of New York electricity created the infrastructure necessary for long-term success; that was up to Edison. After considering his options, he decided to install his electric lines

A mess of wires nearly darkens the sky over Broadway in New York.

in conduits (underground pipes) where they would be safer. The space above the streets was already crowded with a dense, ugly web of telegraph lines that dimmed the sky. However, getting permission from New York City's corrupt bosses to install 80,000 feet (24 km) of underground electrical cable bogged the project down for months.

Meanwhile, Edison received about 3,000 requests for individual systems. He refused all but a few. In the spring of 1880, he electrified a new steamship, the *Columbia*. For the Blue Mountain House resort in the wilderness of the Adirondacks, a dynamo, bulbs, and hardware had to be shipped to the site on the backs of mules. Millionaire backer William Vanderbilt demanded a system for his Fifth Avenue

Street Amusement

Shortly after the Pearl Street station opened, one of Edison's cables at the corner of Nassau and Ann Streets was split by a spike, causing a serious leak that electrified a section of the pavement. Horses passing this corner would suddenly drop to their knees, bolt with their carts rumbling behind them, or rear up uncontrollably. For several days, crowds gathered to watch the equestrian antics, until Edison got word of the leak and fixed it.

mansion. When the system was turned on, however, a small section of wallpaper started smoking, and Mrs. Vanderbilt had the entire installation torn out immediately.

Another individual Edison system was installed at the Manhattan printing company of Hinds & Ketcham. Their business depended on seeing detail and color clearly, and the new light was perfect for the work. They said it was "the best substitute for daylight we have ever known, and almost as cheap."

By 1881, Edison had finally been granted permission to dig in New York—but only at night, so traffic wouldn't be disrupted. It was slow going; by December, only a third of the proposed wiring had been laid.

Around this time, Edison left Menlo Park with his family and moved into a house to live near the Pearl Street Station. He seldom stayed with his family, however. He slept—when he slept—a few feet from the big dynamos.

On April 12, 1882, an Edison demonstration system came online for half a mile (805 meters) along London's

Holborn viaduct. Edison's plant powered street lights and interior lights for shops, homes, and even part of the Royal Post Office. The British press was delighted, but the question remained: Would Edison's larger system in downtown Manhattan be profitable?

Gas lighting companies hoped he would fail. They spread rumors that Edison's lights radiated deadly rays. Edison countered these stories by publishing accounts about people who had been gassed to death and homes that had burned down because of gas lighting.

In preparation for the advent of his electric system, Edison did a complete survey of the business district he would light, detailing when every gas light was used, the number of people in the area, their professions, and the work that might be done by new electric motors. It was one of the first complete

Humming with power, the Pearl Street Station was the world's first large-scale electric power plant.

Lord Kelvin (1824–1907)

Lord Kelvin, born William Thomson, was made a baron by England's Queen Victoria in recognition of the enormous scope of his scientific, mathematical, and engineering discoveries. The Irishman investigated almost every aspect of science, and invented many tools of science. "Kelvin" is now a scientific term for a unit of temperature.

consumer surveys. It showed Edison what his customers really needed.

As always, Edison continued to look for ways to improve his inventions. He knew that his overall system of providing electricity was just as important as the lightbulb, and more revolutionary. Even his basic wiring plan—from dynamo to feeder lines to home circuits—reduced the amount of copper wire the system used to about one eighth of the original estimates, saving hundreds of thousands of dollars. It was remarkably new and entirely simple. British scientist Lord Kelvin was asked why no one else had thought of such a simple solution. He replied, "The only answer I can think of is that no one else is Edison."

Tom Edison was uneasy with satisfaction. He kept working on the lightbulb and developed a filament that lasted even longer. He invented a radically new three-wire system of delivering electricity, which used a third, "neutral" wire to balance current changes and allowed the use of much thinner wire, reducing

"We will make electric light so cheap only the wealthy can afford to burn candles!"

–Thomas Edison to his financial backers

the amount of copper needed by an additional two-thirds. He dismayed his investors by delaying the completion of the system until he had it "just right."

After many tests and adjustments, Edison's Pearl Street Station powered up on September 4, 1882, to illuminate about one square mile (2.6 sq km) of downtown Manhattan for 49 subscribers. It was still a gamble: Every subscribing home had been wired without charge, and Edison had provided his customers free bulbs, along with four months of electricity.

In 1883, the Pearl Street station lost money. By 1884, its subscription list had grown to 455 customers, and it began to make a profit.

Edison wasn't just risking his investors' money. He also invested his own income from his telephone and telegraph patents to start factories to make lamps, dynamos, wiring, and other necessities. In typical Edison style, financial success wasn't the object—it represented a means to fund his curiosity and keep working.

The enormously complex arrangements for financing, manufacturing, shipping, installing, and delivering electricity

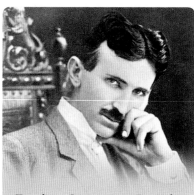

Tesla, Strange Dandy

In many ways, Nikola Tesla was Edison's opposite. He was always spotlessly neat, dressed stylishly, and approached problems theoretically. He was also a tense obsessive-compulsive who counted all his steps so they—like all the numbers in his life—would be divisible by three. Tesla had many phobias: He feared germs most of all, but also stranger things, such as women wearing pearls.

had grown beyond his interest and abilities. And by inventing an industry, he had unwittingly set in motion a war: the War of the Currents.

Nikola Tesla was a Serbian scientist, tall and slim, imperially handsome, with a radiant intelligence and an uncanny understanding of electricity. He had been one of the Boys for a time, but left Edison's laboratory over a dispute. He believed he'd been offered a very large bonus if he could make dynamos work more efficiently. When he greatly increased dynamo output and asked for his payment, Edison said the offer had been a joke. This was probably true, but Tesla wasn't even given a better salary. He quit shortly afterward.

Economic times were hard and the immigrant genius couldn't find another engineering job, so he dug ditches for a while (coincidentally, for Edison's cables).

In 1888, inventor George Westinghouse engaged Tesla to build the electric system he had devised. Unlike Edison's, Westinghouse's system was not based on current flowing evenly through a wire, but on current rapidly changing from plus to minus—an alternating current, or AC.

It's possible that Edison simply didn't have enough mathematical understanding to appreciate the many advantages of alternating current. But it's also possible that his heavy investment in the direct current, or DC, system he'd created prevented him from accepting them.

In the long run, Edison envisioned a DC system based on "neighborhood" generating plants that supplied low-voltage electricity. Direct current couldn't be sent much farther than one mile (1.6 km) without serious loss of current. Indeed, Edison banked on being able to build thousands of these local DC plants.

The voltage of AC, on the other hand, can be changed easily using a transformer, and Tesla appreciated the fact that high-voltage AC could be sent economically over long distances. Instead of thousands of local power plants, AC allowed electricity to be generated efficiently by one distant plant. The high voltage could then be reduced in stages by transformers. Higher voltages could be used for harder work, such as industrial motors or electric railways. Lower voltages could be used for home appliances, which ran best at 110 volts.

There were some advantages to DC electricity, but in promoting his system, Edison seized on what he thought

George Westinghouse was an electrical pioneer with the wisdom to back Nikola Tesla and alternating current.

was a fault of AC: the danger of being killed by an electric shock. Indeed, there was danger in New York's dense banks of aerial wires. Old telegraph wires sometimes fell loose across the high-voltage electric wires used for arc lights, swinging down to jolt pedestrians, or incinerating repair workers in ghastly spectacles above the street.

Edison's lines ran more safely in their underground conduits, and the current at any point in the system was low. But this was largely because DC couldn't be transmitted at high voltage without heavy, expensive wires.

AC current, because of its rapid changes, scrambles nerve messages and may cause a human heart to stop more easily than a DC shock. But the truth is that any electrical current is dangerous. This didn't stop Edison from circulating stories about the awful hazards of AC shock. Edison's employees Harold Brown and Arthur Kennealy publicized these dangers by killing stray dogs and old horses with AC shocks. These stunts reached a disgraceful peak when Topsy, an elephant who had killed her trainer, was fitted with a large electric headpiece and electrocuted.

George Westinghouse, a decent and honorable man, wrote to Edison asking that they meet and reconcile their differences, and perhaps even merge their interests. Edison refused, and then insulted his rival: He suggested that the most humane way to execute criminals might be to use high-voltage AC current, and that the executions be called "westinghousing."

The controversy over "westinghousing" condemned criminals went on until Harold Brown was granted $10,000 to build electric chairs for New York State prisons. (Edison consulted on their design behind the scenes.) On August 6, 1890, ax-murderer William Kemmler was electrocuted using AC current. It was a grisly process. Appalled, George Westinghouse said to the *New York Times,* "I do not care to talk about it. It has been a brutal affair."

In the end, the outcome of the War of the Currents was determined by consumers voting with dollars. In 1889, Westinghouse AC had five times as many customers as Edison DC. Central generation and long-distance transmission were simply more economical. The final battle ended on October 27, 1893, when Westinghouse and Tesla won the contract to harness the power of Niagara Falls to generate alternating current.

Fateful Misstep

Toward the end of his life, Edison admitted that one of his greatest regrets was that he'd underestimated Nikola Tesla as a dandy and a dreamer, and that one of his biggest mistakes was having dismissed alternating current as an efficient way to distribute electric power.

chapter **10**

Making Music

Edison's home life hardly existed. During the search for a workable lightbulb he didn't leave the lab for weeks at a time. On rare Sundays, he would spend some time with Mary and the children, but he would always amble back to the lab in the afternoon.

In truth, Tom Edison only felt at home with the Boys.

A year before her death in 1884, Mary Edison was neglected, heavier, but dressed like a fine lady.

Though he admired beauty in women— he was charmed when the great actress Sarah Bernhardt visited the lab—he had a low opinion of female intellect. "It is very difficult to make women believe anything that is so," he said. "[They] are inclined to be obstinate." He preferred a rough male atmosphere of serious work, chewing tobacco, hard swearing, and horseplay.

The isolation of Menlo Park wore Mary Edison down. She was a simple woman of deep kindness and patience, but she longed for company. She was delighted when the family moved to New York City to be near Pearl Street Station, and she found comfort in being with her family. But she still suffered from headaches and panic attacks. In early 1884, Edison took her on a vacation to Florida where she rested while he hunted and fished. But when she returned to Menlo Park, she fell ill. She died on August 9, 1884, of "brain congestion." The cause of death was later described as typhoid—but it could have been any commonplace infection in that era.

Edison's sons, William Leslie and Thomas Alva Edison, Jr., shown here in 1883, never had a close relationship with their father.

Edison had neglected and lost his only romance. He was struck by grief and frustration. Why couldn't he have invented a way to help Mary? The boys were whisked away to live with relatives, but 12-year-old Dot became Papa's constant companion. She drove him around the countryside in a pony cart. She joined him in the lab, at board meetings, and even at Delmonico's, the elegant New York restaurant.

Thomas Edison had become a brand name for

> *"I looked at this man . . . and I thought of Napoleon."*
>
> –Sarah Bernhardt, after her visit to Menlo Park

invention by the middle of his life, prominent in society and industry. The simple life of Menlo Park was gone. He was surrounded and often hindered by the corporations he'd created around him.

In 1885, while in Boston working on a project, Edison reunited with an old "plug" friend, Ezra Gilliland, who became a close friend and assistant for a time. At Ezra's home, he met

Taking Care of Business

On December 12, 1882, Edison attended a gala opening of the newly electrified Bijou Theater. Gilbert and Sullivan's *Iolanthe* was being performed before an audience of dignitaries when the new lights began to dim. Edison grabbed Edward Johnson, one of the Boys, and headed for the cellar—the boiler fires were low! The two men hung up their tailcoats to shovel coal, then returned to the performance.

Mina Miller, brainy and beautiful, made a confident and alert helpmate for a shy and rumpled "wizard."

a strikingly beautiful, intelligent young woman named Mina Miller. Edison later said he was "staggered" by her. On February 24, 1886, Edison and Mina were married. They spent their honeymoon in Ft. Meyers, Florida, which had become a haven for Edison during stressful times.

Mina was not a shy country girl like Mary but a confident and educated young woman.

Her father was a founder of the Chautauqua Institution, a summer retreat dedicated to religious, intellectual, and artistic education, so she was raised in the company of extraordinary talent. She was a strong, nurturing presence who would play an important part in her husband's life and, to some extent, would smooth his rough exterior.

The couple returned to a mansion Edison had bought for Mina in West Orange, New Jersey. Soon, Edison began work on a new, larger laboratory. He now commanded an army of assistants and researchers in several buildings, where he pursued dozens of projects. He called the employees his "muckers," and he was the "boss mucker."

For some time now, the business of producing electricity had become a bore to Edison. To simplify the work, Edison merged many of his individual corporations into the Edison General Electric Company. Edison GE them merged with an AC competitor,

Edison bought this mansion in West Orange, New Jersey, to live in with his new bride.

the Thomson-Houston Electric Company. Hidden behind this series of mergers was the canny financier, J. P. Morgan. On April 15, 1892, the consolidated corporations became the General Electric Company, which is still a giant corporation today. But Morgan's maneuvering had made Edison and his early backers nothing more than employees of the conglomerate. Edison was a wealthy man but he never realized the spectacular profits Morgan and other money managers wrung out of the industry he'd helped to create.

Between 1883 and 1893, a fountain of invention sprung forth from the mind of Tom Edison. The new lab sent the "boss mucker" skipping from project to project, doing what he loved most: investigating. In 1886, Alexander Graham Bell called Edison's attention back to his favorite invention. With others, Bell had developed a sound-recording device called the graphophone. Instead of tin foil attached to a steel roll, it used wax-coated paper cylinders that could be replaced and replayed. It was a fine idea—but closely related to the phonograph. To avoid legal difficulties, Bell offered Edison a half share in the American Graphophone Company. Edison was insulted. "Under no circumstances will I have anything to do with Graham Bell [or] with his phonograph pronounced backward," he declared. He threw himself into redesigning the phonograph himself, using a similar thick wax cylinder.

A premature—and unsuccessful—demonstration of the new model chased away solid backers. Instead, Edison's

North American Phonograph Company found funding from the less wealthy, less experienced Jesse Lippincott. Edison, always the perfectionist, delayed production of the improved machine for almost a year. When the devices finally came out with the magical Edison name, they sold briskly as office equipment for dictating letters.

Unfortunately, secretaries didn't like to use the new phonographs. They were difficult to keep adjusted. Their batteries were unreliable and (like all acid batteries) dangerous. Edison's recording wax corroded the needles until the machines were unusable. 8,000 machines were returned for repair. Most were junked.

Despite all of this, the cylinders did reproduce sound fairly well, which made many enthusiastic about using the phonograph to play music. But Edison dismissed this use, which he thought made his invention seem more like a toy than a tool.

And yet, Edison was not completely opposed to using technology for fun: the Edison Phonograph Toy Manufacturing Company installed tiny phonographs in dolls so that they "spoke" when a handle was turned. The dolls sold well, but were too delicate to survive shipping.

Edison's office dictating machine was complex, fussy, and ultimately unsuccessful.

Edison kept producing music cylinders long after the public showed a preference for disks.

Very few of the dolls actually talked when they reached their destination.

All in all, nothing demonstrates Edison's failures as a businessman quite as clearly as the phonograph. The mishandling of this invention spread over 40 years. In 1878, Edison's phonograph was a sensation all over the world—but he abandoned the idea. In 1886, he was stung into manufacturing by Bell's offer of a merger—but he ignored manufacturing difficulties, bad batteries, returns, and bad sales. He blamed the failure of his office-dictating machine on lazy office workers. And he avoided music cylinders even after 1889, when nickel-in-a-slot musical phonograph parlors became a sensation across the country.

Eventually, Edison did enter the music business, but reproducing cylinders was tricky. He couldn't yet reproduce many cylinders from a master mold. Instead, each performance was recorded directly onto only half a dozen cylinders! Musicians worked for days, repeating a song over and over, in order to record enough copies to meet demand. In 1892, Berliner Gramophone began selling disk-based recordings that could be stamped from a master disk thousands of times. The disks were were also easier to store and play than cylinders, and Americans seemed to prefer them. But Edison stubbornly stuck with cylinders and found a way to "master" them. By 1912, he was making both disks and cylinders—but his disks played only on Edison machines.

Edison's worst mistake was selecting all the music. His competitors recorded star performers like Paganini, Louis Armstrong, and the great opera tenor Enrico Caruso. Edison recorded unknown musicians

An early concept of the phonograph as concert-house entertainment was promising, but didn't work out.

for low fees. The deaf Edison wouldn't record jazz, choosing mainly old fashioned songs, instead. Then he blamed the public for choosing "bad music."

In 1929, Edison got out of the music business. Radio had cut into profits, and the inventor of the phonograph had been pushed aside by companies that listened to their customers.

Almost Wireless

Edison came close to inventing wireless communication when he created a "space telegraph" to send messages from moving trains to wires beside the track. Messages could travel up to three miles (5 km) with a similar device he invented for ships. Edison dropped these lines of investigation, but later regretted it when the inventors of radio built on his work.

chapter 11

Gold Mine to Silver Screen

Edison's mind was like a crow, picking up anything shiny. Gold was very shiny. On a trip to Colorado in 1878, he became interested in using electricity to locate gold and silver deposits. He'd found some gold when looking for rare metals for the perfect lamp filament. Then, in 1879, he formed the Edison Ore Milling Company to extract gold dust from gold-mine tailings, the rock dug out of the ground to make a mine shaft. Edison reasoned that a magnet placed beside a falling stream of crushed tailings should pull iron into one hopper, while gold, unaffected by the magnet, should drop directly into another. But the amount of gold he retrieved was tiny.

In 1880, he used his magnetic process to extract rich iron ore from the iron sands of Rhode Island. The process worked well but, unexpectedly, the heat of commercial furnaces wouldn't melt the fine iron-ore dust. The operation shut down in 1882.

Edison's plan to magnet-mine low-grade iron ore was a long and expensive folly that never paid off.

ORE

An ore is a natural mineral containing a desired substance, such as iron or silver.

Edison's miners dug ore to feed a complex of crushers, separators, and furnaces.

In June 1887, Edison tried a new gold-extraction process. His experiments failed—but renewed his interest in iron. Cast iron and steel were always in demand. If magnetic separation could enrich the low-grade ores he'd found in upstate New Jersey, he could make a fortune!

Edison threw himself into iron milling with happy obsession. He even moved up to the mine for five years, blissfully supervising the gritty work and the operation of his machines, including a remarkable series of conveyor belts. (These belts probably influenced the automobile production line that would later work so well for Henry Ford.) He loved the company of his miners and mechanics and the rough life of the site.

Between 1887 and 1898, Edison poured millions of his own money into the milling business, selling off almost all of his stock in General Electric. Then, richer, more easily mined iron-ore deposits were discovered around Lake Superior, and Edison's expensive New Jersey operation couldn't compete. A friend pointed out what the GE stock would have been worth if Edison hadn't sold it. Edison replied, "It's gone, but we had a [heck] of a time spending it."

In 1888, George Eastman, another visionary inventor, started selling the first personal camera, the Kodak. The ads

declared, "You push the button; we do the rest." The owner took pictures, sent the camera back to Eastman's company, and received a camera with new film along with their printed photographs. Edison bought one immediately.

Around this time, Edison was visited by Eadweard Muybridge, a photographer who had developed ways to take multiple photos of moving people and animals. He had plans for an image-projecting machine, and proposed to combine the device with Edison's phonograph. Edison declined politely; he was already working on a way to record motion the way his phonograph recorded sound.

One of Edison's muckers, William Dickson, was a photographer. He helped Edison develop a pair of complex machines that strained even the great inventor's mechanical genius: the kinetograph (a camera to record motion) and the kinetoscope (a device to show motion). For the camera, Dickson had Eastman create a long, thin roll of his celluloid photographic film. Edison then developed machinery to run the film past the lens, stopping it briefly every time the lens shutter opened—40 times a second! In this way, the kinetograph could record motion. There had never been anything like it.

Lights, camera, elephant! Film pioneer Eadward Muybridge created these sequential photographs of animal motion.

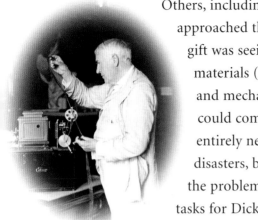

Others, including Muybridge, had approached the idea—but Edison's gift was seeing how existing materials (like Eastman's film) and mechanics (like the camera) could combine into something entirely new. Early models were disasters, but Edison identified the problems and sketched out tasks for Dickson.

Edison examines a strip of film for the kinetoscope.

Then he left for Paris to show off some of his inventions at the Universal Exhibition of 1889. In France, Edison was greeted as a colleague by intellectual giants such as Louis Pasteur and Marie Curie, and was given a diploma of honor and five gold medals.

When he returned to West Orange, Dickson was eager to show him something. Edison sat and watched as an image of Dickson lit up a white screen, tipped its hat, and said, "Good morning, Mr. Edison, glad to see you back. I hope you are satisfied with the kineto-phonograph."

Edison displays at the Universal Exhibition covered an acre of the site and included telephone switchboards, electric dynamos, and a fantastic show of electric lights.

Dickson had succeeded! But Edison felt that combining sound and pictures on a large scale wasn't

practical, and the talking-film project was put aside. Instead, he concentrated on creating a one-person silent-movie viewer, encouraged by the financial success of nickel-in-a-slot phonograph parlors. Dickson was told to get a viewer ready for the World's Columbian Exposition of 1893 in Chicago, but the fair came and went as Edison tinkered with his machine.

Edison had high-minded ideas about the kinetograph. Like others, Dickson realized it was an opportunity for lots of fun. Dickson built the first movie studio, "Black Maria," on Edison's West Orange property. The structure was covered in black-tar paper, and rotated on a circular track, following the sun for the best lighting. He made films of cockfights, dancing ladies, circus acts, and other crowd-pleasing shows.

On April 14, 1894, the first kinetoscope parlor opened in New York City to instant success. Soon, film reels were lengthened to a full minute. When a boxing ring was reduced to fit inside Black Maria,

Edison's film studio, clad in dark tar paper, resembled a type of jail wagon called a "Black Maria."

The Great Train Robbery

One of Edison's first full-length Vitascope features was a western, filmed on location along the Lackawanna Railroad in New Jersey. *The Great Train Robbery* ran 10 minutes and had 14 scenes. It was the first thriller, with chases, shootouts, and other action-packed scenes. Gilbert M. "Broncho Billy" Anderson, who played three roles, became the first cowboy star.

filmed matches became an audience favorite.

Dickson was still interested in projecting film onto a screen, but Edison stubbornly believed he could make more money with the small-scale kinetoscope. Dickson started working with other inventors on a projection machine, but he had trouble producing enough light for the images to be clearly seen. When Edison discovered that his employee had been working with "rivals," he was furious and fired the young man who had taken the project so far.

Eventually, Edison's kinetoscope distributors insisted on a machine that would show the images on a large screen for an audience. In France, Thomas Armat had created the Phantascope, which achieved a clear projection by duplicating the kinetograph camera's trick: It stopped each image briefly as the light was projected through it. The distributors offered to promote Edison as the inventor instead of Armat, for a fee. Edison agreed, and the new

The Vitascope was an entertainment marvel: a motion-picture projector for a large audience.

projector, renamed the Vitascope, premiered in April 1896. Audiences were delighted. They saw dances, a comic battle between Uncle Sam and the British John Bull, and the first close-up of a man kissing a woman. During Vitascope's first week in Los Angeles, 20,000 people saw the show. Another 10,000 were turned away.

In 1895, Edison took a break from his other work to examine the wonder of X-rays. These mysterious rays had been discovered that year by William Röntgen of the Netherlands. Röntgen found that a current of electricity in a device called a Crookes tube created an invisible light that passed through flesh but not bone—leaving the image of a person's skeleton on a photographic plate. It was also possible to shine X-rays through a limb onto a fluorescent screen to see a live picture of the bones beneath the surface.

Edison's brief motion picture of *The Kiss* wowed audiences.

The latter technology especially interested Edison. He and his muckers tried 8,000 chemical compounds in pursuit of a better screen. Finally, Edison telegraphed Lord Kelvin, "Calcium tungstate properly crystallized gives splendid fluorescence . . . rendering photographs unnecessary."

The mystery of this phenomenon fascinated Edison for months. He built many fluoroscopes—boxes with peepholes through which X-ray images could be viewed. He sent his machines to surgeons and hospitals, allowing them to detect bone fractures and metal fragments in wounds. He even demonstrated a fluoroscope at the Electrical Exposition of 1896 in New York, allowing visitors to view their own hands or feet.

Edison became more cautious when the fluoroscope seriously harmed his eyesight. But it was already too late for his assistant, Clarence Dally; X-ray exposure gave him what we now know as radiation poisoning. He died in 1904, after having both arms amputated. Edison's X-ray work had advanced medicine significantly, but progress did not come without a price.

The fluoroscope's constant stream of X-rays was revealing but toxic.

chapter 12
The Age of Edison

Thomas Edison had helped usher in a new age—an age of science and technology, of light, electricity, and recorded sound. Now, as the country moved into the 20th century, a new age was dawning: the age of speed. The bicycle craze of the 1890s had given over to the automobile craze. Edison was a keen observer, and he saw that the horse would soon be obsolete. His own life had been defined by

A "box of electricity" was the goal for the West Orange muckers in pursuing a working storage battery.

electricity, so it was understandable that Edison thought the automobile should run on electricity.

Unfortunately, the familiar liquid-acid batteries were wrong for the electric car. When they were exhausted, they had to be refilled with new chemicals. Edison wanted a battery that could be recharged from an electric source, a "box of electricity."

He and his muckers began thousands of experiments. One promising battery was created and sold in 1903.

But when it was installed in cars, it leaked. Edison recalled all the batteries at his own expense and shut down production until the nickel-iron alkaline battery could be perfected.

During this period Edison met one of his managers at the Detroit Edison Company, a young man named Henry Ford. As the two men spoke, Ford described his ideas about producing a widely available car. Edison was enthusiastic and helpful. It was the start of a lifelong friendship.

In 1909 production began on Edison's revised, improved battery. It was not an ideal battery for electric cars, but it was a great success in many other areas and continues to be a standby for rugged use. (In both world wars, it was the primary battery for submarines.)

In 1912 Henry Ford decided to equip his Model T car with a self-starter, replacing the labor-intensive crank mechanism used previously. He collaborated with Edison on the starter, dynamo, wiring, and battery. Edison's alkaline battery wasn't adaptable to the self-starter, but working together, Ford and Edison succeeded in taking some of the mess and muscle out

Early electric cars were prized for their simplicity, reliability—and lack of starting crank!

of starting a car. And Edison's work on batteries had made him financially sound again.

Edison benefited from former follies. As a canny observer of changing culture, he foresaw a building boom using a new material, reinforced concrete. He investigated the key ingredient of concrete, Portland cement: a mixture of clay and crushed limestone heated in big kilns. Then it occurred to him that the massive machinery he'd built for crushing rocks at his failed ironworks was perfect for crushing limestone to make cement.

The gigantic ore-milling rollers pulverized limestone with ease. The conveyer-belt system took the rock to finer and finer crushers and sifting meshes, then to a new kind of moving kiln, 150 feet (46 m) long by 9 feet (3 m) wide. The works produced a superior cement at a rate of 1,110 barrels a day—more than five times the output of most competitors.

Edison built several "fireproof" concrete buildings as part of his factory complex in West Orange. With the welfare of factory workers in mind, he also designed a concrete house. The two-story cottage of six rooms made good housing affordable—it cost just $300 in 1908. Edison's system of

Using interlocking molds, Edison could produce a cheap and sturdy house in just three days.

sectional cast-iron molds poured the structure over the course of 12 hours. In three days, the molds came apart to reveal a complete dwelling, ready for windows and doors, with built-in conduits for wiring, plumbing, and heating.

Edison created a variety of concrete furniture, including these phonograph cabinets.

Edison was right about the need for concrete—his cement mills made money. He was wrong about concrete homes—the public wasn't ready for them. Only a few homes were completed, in addition to a gardener's cottage and garage for Edison's own house. Edison loved concrete. He designed furniture, pianos, and even phonograph cabinets made of poured concrete stained to wood or marble colors. The most impressive structure his concrete built, however, was the original Yankee Stadium.

On December 7, 1914, an explosion in the concrete film-finishing lab at West Orange started an enormous blaze that spread to other structures. The concrete wasn't flammable, but the building's contents—Vitascope film, phonograph records, and other combustibles—went up with a terrible roar that melted the floors, caved in the walls, and destroyed most of his lab. Edison shook his head and joked with the firemen and his muckers, "Although I am over 67 years old, I'll start all over again tomorrow." And he did.

Edison and Ford

Ford and Edison admired each other but had different personalities. Edison, in his late sixties, was mellow, humorous, contemplative. Ford, in his mid-fifties, was sharp, quick, and hyperactive, with a nasty temper and a streak of outright prejudice. Edison addressed Ford as "Henry." Ford addressed him as "Mr. Edison."

The disastrous fire placed Edison and his muckers in real financial danger. Luckily, help soon came from a close friend, Henry Ford. Ford's regard for Edison had grown over the years, and he now advanced Edison large sums and loaned him even more to help him rebuild. Ford regarded Edison as a national treasure, and refused to let him sink.

The friendship comforted both men. Years before, Edison had bought a vacation home called Seminole Lodge in Fort Myers, Florida. He induced Ford to buy a place nearby. They took their first camping trip together in 1914, stalking through the Florida Everglades with the naturalist John Burroughs, who taught them about birds, plants, and woodcraft. This led to an almost yearly series of camping jaunts. Edison, Ford, Burroughs, and tire manufacturer Harvey Firestone called themselves the Four Vagabonds and rumbled through the backroads of

the Northeast in open cars, followed by a truck caravan of
secretaries, chefs, mechanics, and equipment.

The Vagabonds shared Edison's talent for being a boy.
Every night, they would sit around a fire and tell stories, sing,
and relax. If a car broke down, Ford and Edison would climb
out and fix it. Edison was quiet; he often read or simply
napped on the grass. Ford, more active, chopped firewood or
competed with Firestone in mowing long grass with scythes.
As the trips grew more famous, and more reporters started
to follow them, they were joined occasionally by other
celebrities. Even President Warren G. Harding paid them a
visit. At first, Edison thought the he was just a city slicker,
but he was won over when the president
offered him a chew of his tobacco.

President Warren G.
Harding relaxes with the
Vagabonds on one of the
their summer rambles.

Burroughs wrote, "It was a great pleasure to see Edison relax and turn vagabond so easily, sleeping in his clothes and dropping off to sleep like a baby, getting up to replenish the fire at daylight or before, making his toilet at the wayside creek or pool."

In 1914 the talk around the campfire centered on the Great War raging in Europe. Although the United States had not yet entered the conflict, many thought its involvement was inevitable. Back at home Edison—always good for a newspaper story—gave his own opinion of America's situation. He felt that the country was unprepared for war and didn't have a body of scientific advisors like Germany's. He insisted that the country should prepare for the worst and build up its defense capabilities. "We haven't any troops, we haven't any ammunition, we are an unorganized mob," he stated. If the country needed his inventive skill, he would gladly serve.

In July 1915, Edison was asked to head the Naval Consulting Board of scientists and inventors, dedicated to helping the country prepare for war. When German submarines began sinking ships carrying Americans, Edison addressed the problem immediately. He asked for a chart showing all reported sinkings to

"It was a great pleasure to see Edison relax and turn vagabond so easily."

–John Burroughs

Edison stands front and center with the Naval Consulting Board in 1915.

determine a pattern of operation. The U.S. Navy had no such chart, but the British Navy supplied one. Edison used it to devise routes that avoided submarine attack.

America finally entered World War I in 1917. During the course of the conflict, Edison presented 45 inventions to the Navy. Deeply suspicious of change and outsiders, the Navy pigeonholed every one of them. Edison's most lasting contribution to the national defense was his tenacious battle to establish a Naval Research Laboratory to pursue advances in military technology. It was built too late for World War I, but it was responsible for technical advances that helped the U.S. Navy prepare for World War II.

During this time, Mina was an almost constant

World War I

World War I was a global conflict spurred by a local event. When Archduke Franz Ferdinand of Austria was assassinated, his government turned to Serbia for retribution. But the dispute didn't end there: The countries of Europe were tied together by numerous treaties of alliance, which now compelled them to choose sides and act. By the war's end, 16 million soldiers and civilians died.

Edison enjoys his 84th birthday in Fort Myers, as always protected and nurtured by Mina.

companion, even as Edison carried out torpedo-detection experiments on a boat offshore. She suffered from seasickness but wrote to their daughter, "father was the only consideration." Edison was later offered a Distinguished Service Medal for his contribution to the war effort, but he refused it, saying that others had done more.

After the war, Edison didn't take much time to relax. In fact, the war had made him aware of a problem that would be of increasing importance in the modern world: Any world conflict could interrupt the nation's supply of essential materials. Today, oil is the commodity most often affected. For Edison, it was rubber. And so he began his last obsessive investigation: searching for a domestic source of rubber.

By 1928, Edison had tested 14,000 native plants and found rubber in 600 of them. He started focusing on goldenrod (which contained about five percent rubber), then noted the best varieties. Edison admired the botanist Luther Burbank, who bred edible plants, and used his methods to "breed up" goldenrod into a giant variety that reached 14 feet (4 m) tall and contained 12 percent rubber.

Unfortunately, it was an inferior grade of rubber, and synthetic rubber made from petroleum was already starting to replace natural varieties. But Edison quietly continued his investigation. When visitors inquired about the project, he said, "We are just beginning."

Despite his indomitable drive to work, Edison's health was declining, and the nation realized it would soon lose its "most useful citizen." Awards and honors poured in, and Edison took them with a twinkling eye, some of his old wit, and considerable grace. On May 21, 1928, he was awarded the Congressional Gold Medal. Treasury secretary Andrew Mellon came to the Edison laboratory to make the presentation.

In 1929, GE began to anticipate the 50th anniversary of Edison's lightbulb and asked him to be part of the Golden Jubilee of Light in Schenectady, New York. Edison had no love for J. P. Morgan's GE and didn't want to take part. But Henry Ford's historic village was nearing completion, so Ford

On an afternoon away from the lab, the aging Edison relaxes on his West Orange lawn.

"kidnapped" the entire affair and brought it to Dearborn, Michigan, along with a willing Edison.

Edison had almost died of pneumonia in August but arrived by train on October 21 and shuffled dutifully through the ceremony for Ford's sake. Afterward Mina took him back home to West Orange, where his health continued to decline.

Thomas Alva Edison died on October 18, 1931. When doctors told him he would never return to work, he seemed to lose interest in living. Just before he lapsed into a peaceful coma, Mina leaned over him and spoke close to his ear, "Are you suffering?"

"No," he replied, "just waiting."

Edison didn't believe in heaven. He only believed that the atoms of his body would be recycled, by and by, into natural materials. Nature was his god, and it was enough for him. Years earlier, when he was pursuing an efficient battery, he said, "I don't think Nature would be so unkind as to withhold the secret of a good storage battery, if a real earnest hunt were made for it. I'm going to hunt." For him, nature was a benign and divine mystery, a kind of playground.

Some critics have said that Edison's assistants did most of his work. Of course, the Boys were always an important part of the process—but what work would they have done without his spark, his guidance, or his cheery confidence that an answer would appear?

Many of the things we celebrate as Edison's inventions were first conceived by someone else: the dynamo, the storage battery, even the lightbulb. But he made them work and gave them to the world.

In many ways, Edison invented invention. Bell Labs, NASA, Los Alamos, Jet Propulsion Laboratory, the Naval Research Laboratory, and countless modern research institutions that pursue organized, focused, fact-based results, owe a debt to Menlo Park.

Edison confounded every label. He was warm and humorous, cold and spiteful, a wonderful friend, a distant father, a genius, and a rube. He loved publicity, but was painfully shy. He loved the company of his Boys and muckers, but a part of him was always aloof. He talked easily with great men in high places, and spit tobacco juice on the lab floor with mechanics and carpenters.

Thomas Alva Edison: inventor, scientist, boss mucker, plug, wizard.

There are thousands of photographs of Edison's face, but the real man is elusive, hiding. We can't really know him, even though he's our almost constant companion. When we flick on a light, type an e-mail, listen to music, Thomas Edison is with us.

Events in the Life of Thomas Edison

August 1869
Edison begins work at the Gold Indicator Company in New York City.

October 21, 1879
The first practical electric lightbulb is demonstrated to the press.

February 11, 1847
Thomas Alva Edison is born in Milan, Ohio.

Winter 1859
Edison quits school to become a candy butcher and newsboy.

March 1877
Edison invents the carbon button microphone, making the telephone a practical instrument.

August 9, 1884
Mary Stilwell Edison dies.

December 25, 1871
Edison marries his employee, Mary Stilwell.

1854
The Edison family moves to Port Huron, Michigan.

July 18, 1878
Edison invents the phonograph.

March 26, 1876
The Menlo Park lab opens.

August 1862
Edison begins learning telegraphy.

February 24, 1886
Edison marries
Mina Miller.

1891
A 10-year project begins
to separate iron ore
electromagnetically.

July 7, 1915
Edison is named
head of the Naval
Consulting Board for
defense inventions.

October 6, 1889
The first synchronized
projection of cinema
and sound takes place
at West Orange.

April 14, 1894
The first Edison
kinetograph parlor
opens in New York City.

October 21, 1929
The "Golden
Jubilee of Light" is
held at Dearborn
Village, Michigan.

December 1887
Edison's laboratories
move to West Orange,
New Jersey.

August 3, 1914
World War I begins.

August 26, 1910
Edison demonstrates
the Kinetophone's
moving pictures
with sound.

October 18, 1931
Thomas Alva
Edison dies in
West Orange,
New Jersey.

Summer 1906
Edison's cement plant is
built using crushers from the
unsuccessful iron-ore plant.

For Further Study

One of the great treasures of Rutgers University in New Jersey is their collection of Edison's papers—notes, lab journals, letters, articles—the depth is overwhelming. The collection is digitized online and has excellent timelines that will help any student place the events of Edison's life and work in sequence: http://edison.rutgers.edu/

The About.com:inventors series has a good overview of Edison's work: http://inventors.about.com/library/inventors/bledison.htm

Wikipedia's coverage of Edison is respectful of his great place in the shaping the modern world but is not simple hero worship, and it has good links to other sites on specific topics: http://en.wikipedia.org/wiki/Thomas_Edison

The Library of Congress website featuring Edison focuses on their collection of sound and film recordings, but the timeline is excellent and some of the clips are entertaining: http://memory.loc.gov/ammem/edhtml/edhome.html

The National Park Service's Edison site has a concise, simple biography: http://www.nps.gov/archive/edis/edisonia/tae_bio.html

Works Cited

P7 "And Edison said…" "Edison: Last Days of the Wizard"

P7 "I am tired of all the glory…" "Edison: Last Days of the Wizard"

P7 "To find a man who has not benefited…" *Thomas A. Edison Album*

P8 "What about the other five…" "Edison: Last Days of the Wizard"

P8 "lived in utter disregard…" *Tesla: Master of Lightning*

P14 "I don't know…Why don't…" *Thomas A. Edison Album*

P15 "My father thought I was stupid…" *Thomas A. Edison Album*

P17 "I did not have my mother long…" *Thomas A. Edison Album*

P17,18 "My mother was the making…" *Edison*

P18 "He spent the greater part…" *Edison*

P18 "I can still remember… *Edison*

P19 "He will blow us all up!" *Edison*

P24 "My refuge was…" *Edison*

P24 "I didn't read a few…" *Edison*

P31 "wide open…" *Edison: A Life of Invention*

P32 "If there was anything…" *Thomas A. Edison Album*

P33 "Say, young man…" *Thomas A. Edison Album*

P36 "I was a ghastly…" *Thomas A. Edison Album*

P37 "Young man, if there is…" *Thomas A. Edison Album*

P37 "It was a lesson to me…" *Thomas A. Edison Album*

P39 "mode of transmission…" *Edison*

P39 "would hereafter devote…" *Edison*

P41 "Fix it!…" *Thomas A. Edison Album*

P42 "How much?…" *Edison: A Life of Invention*

P45 "The memory of her…" *Thomas A. Edison Album,* 52

P47 "What do you think of me…" *Edison,* 98

P47 "after things were going…" *Thomas A. Edison Album,* 56

P48 "Tom, what are you doing?…" *Edison,* 99

P48 "My wife Popsy-Wopsy…" *Thomas A. Edison Album*

P49 "often slept with a revolver…" *Edison*

P52 "Edison's ingenuity…" *Edison*

P56 "which, by the way…" *Edison*, 109

P61 "Edison made your work…" *Thomas Alva Edison, An American Myth*, 38

P63 "laboratory that never sleeps" *Thomas A. Edison Album*

P63 "Genius is one percent…" *Thomas A. Edison Album*

P67 "Haloo!" *Edison: A Life of Invention*

P67 "Mary had a little lamb…" *Edison*, 163

P68 "I was never so…" *Edison*, 163

P68 "the machine began…" *Edison*, 163

P71 "Yes, this is my baby…" *Edison*, 171

P72 "1. Letter Writing…" *North American Review*

P73 "I can never find the thing…" *Thomas Alva Edison, An American Myth*, 153

P76 "I believe I can beat you…" *Edison*, 178

P77 "I start where…" *Makers of the Modern World*, 227

P79 "If it will burn that number…" *Thomas A. Edison Album*, 82

P82 "Nothing that's good…" *Thomas A. Edison Album*, 85

P82 "Edison is one of the most…" *The Wizard of Menlo Park*, 104

P82 "We hope that he…" *Edison*, 206

P86 "the best substitute…" *The Wizard of Menlo Park*, 125

P88 "The only answer I can…" *Edison*, 231

P89 "We will make electric…" *Edison*, 85

P93 "I do not care to talk…" *Empires of Light*, 213

P94 "It is very difficult…" *Edison*, 285

P95 "I looked at this man…: *Edison*, 245

P98 "Under no circumstances…" *The Wizard of Menlo Park*, 157

P103 "it's gone but we had…" *Edison: A Life of Invention*, 339

P105 "Good morning, Mr. Edison…" *The Wizard of Menlo Park*, 196

P109 "Calcium tungstate properly…" *Edison: A Life of Invention*, 311

P111 "I know several thousand…" *Edison*, 413

P116 "It was a great pleasure…" *Edison*, 461

P117 "We haven't any" *Edison*, 446

P120 "Are you suffering?" *Edison*, 452

P120 "I don't think Nature…" *Edison*, 407

Bibliography

Cheney & Uth, *Tesla: Master of Lightning;* 1999, Barnes & Noble.

Edison, Thomas A., "The Phonograph and Its Future," Cedar Falls, IA, *North American Review,* June, 1878.

Frost, Lawrence A., *Thomas A. Edison Album,* Seattle, Superior Publishing Company, 1969.

Israel, Paul, *Edison: A Life Of Invention,* Hoboken, John Wiley & Sons, Inc., 1998.

Jonnes, Jill, *Empires of Light,* New York, Random House, Inc., 2003.

Josephson, Matthew, "EDISON: Last Days of the Wizard," *American Heritage Magazine;* 1959 6, p32.

Josephson, Matthew, *Edison;* New York, McGraw-Hill, 1959.

Stross, Randall, *The Wizard of Menlo Park,* New York, Three Rivers Press, 2007.

Untermeyer, Louis, *Makers of the Modern World: The Lives of Ninety-two Writers, Artists, Scientists, Statesmen, Inventors, Philosophers, Composers, and Other Creators who Formed the Pattern of Our Century,* New York, Simon & Schuster, 1955.

Wachhorst, Wyn, *Thomas Alva Edison, An American Myth,* Cambridge, MIT Press, 1982.

Index

Acknowledgments

I owe many people for the pleasure of examining Edison's life. Among them are my agent Susan Cohen, my DK editor Beth Hester, my friend and benefactor Laura Schifrin, my supportive and indispensable children, Sally, Web and Sam, and Rutgers scholar Louis Carlat. For my pedagogic outlook I owe much to my small Irregulars: Max, Lucas, Alder, River, the Dread Red Pirate Davis, Hannah Rose, Mairev and Julianna.

Picture Credits

FRONT COVER Photo by Getty Images/Roger Viollet. Back Cover Photo by The Henry Ford

All the photographs in this book are used with permission and through the courtesy of:

The Henry Ford: pp.1, 4-5, 6, 13T, 61, 62, 122TR, 122BRB

Edison National Historic Site: pp.2, 9, 10(both), 14T, 21, 23, 24, 25, 33, 34, 36, 37, 38, 44, 46, 48(all), 50, 55, 63, 65, 68, 70, 78, 83, 9495, 96, 99, 103, 105T&B, 106, 110, 112, 113, 117, 119, 122BC, 123(all top), 123BLB

Milan Historical Museum: p.11

Getty Images: pp.13B, 122TL Visions of America/Joe Sohm; pp.41, 122TC artpartner-images; pp.53, 64, 92, 111 Getty Images; p.88 Time & Life Pictures; pp.121, 123BR Roger Viollet

Port Huron Museum: pp.14B, 15, 122BLT

Edison Birthplace Museum: pp.16, 122BRT

North Wind Picture Archives: pp.18, 26, 27, 69, 87, 122BLB

Library of Congress: pp.20, 22, 28, 101, 104, 108T, 114, 115, 123BC

Corbis: pp.43, 56, 75, 90, 109, Bettman; p.59 Araldo de Luca; p.76 Schenectady Museum; pp.102, 118 Corbis

DK Images: pp.51, 74 Clive Streeter/The Science Museum, London

Alamy Images: p.79 Daniel Dempster; p.97 Visions of America, LLC; p.100 John Henshall; p.123BTL

New York Daily Graphic 1879: p.81

Harper's Weekly 1882: p.84

Consolidated Edison Company of New York: p.85

Photofest: pp.107, 108B

BORDER IMAGES from left to right: *The Henry Ford, Library of Congress, Edison National Historic Site, Edison National Historic Site, Edison National Historic Site, The Henry Ford*

About the Author

Jan Adkins is the author and illustrator of more than 40 books, most of them non-fiction for young people, his special audience. He is an explainer and storyteller who hikes and sails around the San Francisco Bay area. He's an odd duck, and probably belongs in 1895. You can find more about him at www.janadkins.com.

Other DK Biographies you'll enjoy:

Abigail Adams
Kem Knapp Sawyer
978-0-7566-5209-8 paperback
978-0-7566-5208-1 hardcover

Marie Curie
Vicki Cobb
ISBN 978-0-7566-3831-3 paperback
ISBN 978-0-7566-3832-0 hardcover

Charles Darwin
David C. King
ISBN 978-0-7566-2554-2 paperback
ISBN 978-0-7566-2555-9 hardcover

Princess Diana
Joanne Mattern
ISBN 978-0-7566-1614-4 paperback
ISBN 978-0-7566-1613-7 hardcover

Amelia Earhart
Tanya Lee Stone
ISBN 978-0-7566-2552-8 paperback
ISBN 978-0-7566-2553-5 hardcover

Albert Einstein
Frieda Wishinsky
ISBN 978-0-7566-1247-4 paperback
ISBN 978-0-7566-1248-1 hardcover

Benjamin Franklin
Stephen Krensky
ISBN 978-0-7566-3528-2 paperback
ISBN 978-0-7566-3529-9 hardcover

Gandhi
Amy Pastan
ISBN 978-0-7566-2111-7 paperback
ISBN 978-0-7566-2112-4 hardcover

Harry Houdini
Vicki Cobb
ISBN 978-0-7566-1245-0 paperback
ISBN 978-0-7566-1246-7 hardcover

Helen Keller
Leslie Garrett
ISBN 978-0-7566-0339-7 paperback
ISBN 978-0-7566-0488-2 hardcover

Thomas Jefferson
Jacqueline Ching
ISBN 978-0-7566-4506-9 paperback
ISBN 978-0-7566-4505-2 hardcover

Joan of Arc
Kathleen Kudlinksi
ISBN 978-0-7566-3526-8 paperback
ISBN 978-0-7566-3527-5 hardcover

John F. Kennedy
Howard S. Kaplan
ISBN 978-0-7566-0340-3 paperback
ISBN 978-0-7566-0489-9 hardcover

Martin Luther King, Jr.
Amy Pastan
ISBN 978-0-7566-0342-7 paperback
ISBN 978-0-7566-0491-2 hardcover

Abraham Lincoln
Tanya Lee Stone
ISBN 978-0-7566-0834-7 paperback
ISBN 978-0-7566-0833-0 hardcover

Nelson Mandela
Lenny Hort & Laaren Brown
ISBN 978-0-7566-2109-4 paperback
ISBN 978-0-7566-2110-0 hardcover

Mother Teresa
Maya Gold
ISBN 978-0-7566-3880-1 paperback
ISBN 978-0-7566-3881-8 hardcover

Annie Oakley
Chuck Wills
ISBN 978-0-7566-2997-7 paperback
ISBN 978-0-7566-2986-1 hardcover

Pelé
Jim Buckley
ISBN 978-0-7566-2987-8 paperback
ISBN 978-0-7566-2996-0 hardcover

Eleanor Roosevelt
Kem Knapp Sawyer
ISBN 978-0-7566-1496-6 paperback
ISBN 978-0-7566-1495-9 hardcover

George Washington
Lenny Hort
ISBN 978-0-7566-0835-4 paperback
ISBN 978-0-7566-0832-3 hardcover

Laura Ingalls Wilder
Tanya Lee Stone
ISBN 978-0-7566-4508-3 paperback
ISBN 978-0-7566-4507-6 hardcover

Look what the critics are saying about DK Biography!

"…highly readable, worthwhile overviews for young people…" —*Booklist*

"This new series from the inimitable DK Publishing brings together the usual brilliant photography with a historian's approach to biography subjects." —*Ingram Library Services*